Seminar on the Acquisition of Latin American Library Materials

Bibliography and Reference Series, 33

Laura Gutiérrez-Witt
Executive Secretary

Barbara G. Valk
Chair, Editorial Board

Posters
of the Cuban Diaspora

A Bibliography

Esperanza B. de Varona

SALALM Secretariat
General Library, University of New Mexico
Albuquerque, New Mexico

SALALM Sponsoring Members

University of California, Los Angeles Research Library
Columbia University Libraries
Cornell University Library
Harvard College Library
Haworth Press
University of Illinois, Urbana, Library
University of New Mexico General Libraries
The New York Public Library
University of North Carolina at Chapel Hill
University Libraries
University of Pittsburgh Hillman Library
Princeton University Library
University of Southern California University Libraries
Stanford University Library
University of Texas at Austin General Libraries
Yale University Libraries

2nd Printing February 2002
SALALM Secretariat
Benson Latin American Collection, The University of Texas at Austin

CONTENTS

ACKNOWLEDGEMENTS

I would like to thank the following people for their continuous support in this endeavor:

John McMinn, Floridiana and University Collection Cataloger.

Ana Rosa Núñez, Foreign Languages Bibliographer (Spanish and Portuguese) and Reference Librarian.

Regina Mendoza, student assistant in the Archives and Special Collections Department.

PREFACE

A poster is a work of applied art. It sends a message with brevity and impact, the visual or plastic elements dominating the text. The poster is the simplest and most direct way to deliver an idea to great masses of people. From Honoré Daumier, who created the first illustrated poster in black and white in 1864 and Jules Chéret, a French lithographer who used new methods to design the first colored poster in 1886, to Henri Toulouse-Lautrec, the great French painter of the second half of the nineteenth century who brought his original ideas into this form of design, posters have placed art at the service of advertising and as such have become a powerful propaganda medium.

When Fidel Castro seized power in Cuba in 1959 a massive exodus of the Cuban people began and still continues today. Throughout the history of the Cuban diaspora the poster has played an important role in representing the non-written history of a people in exile. It has invaded the universal mass media as a form of Cuban expression, recording the cultural, political, and economic aspects of the lives of the Cuban exiles as well as their sports activities, music, and art. Far from the "publicity telegram" definition of the poster given by Adolphe Mouron, better known as A.M. Cassandre, the posters of the Cuban diaspora are, as poetically described by Dino Vilani, more like "paper sirens" that help to define the Cuban experience in a foreign land.

The poster is an identity that lives now and forever. It is an eternal instant. When the first poster by Toulouse-Lautrec appeared, Thadee Natanson declared that "this miracle will not be repeated." He pointed out that a poster was "not made to yellow in libraries, but to be stuck on a wall, to become torn and rain-splashed." In his view, the poster is an ephemeral material, yet if he were entirely correct, how many facts of historical value would be lost!

The poster collection in the Cuban Archives of the University of Miami represent efforts to preserve and transmit the Cuban cultural heritage to future generations, providing historical sources for the Cubans of a future free Cuba, Cuban-Americans, and generations of Cubans born in foreign lands about the hopes and aspirations of the Cuban diaspora during the second half of the twentieth century. The need to disseminate information about this important collection inspired the compilation of the following bibliography.

Esperanza B. de Varona

INTRODUCTION

The bibliography lists 542 posters received in the Cuban Archives of the University of Miami Library through March 1992. Many of the posters have been collected by Cuban librarians at the University over nearly four decades. The bulk of the collection, however, has been donated. Two of the most outstanding donations are those from Mercy-Díaz Miranda of *The Miami Herald* and from Agrupación Abdala, a Cuban exile student association.

Among the most important posters in the collection are those designed to promote the Carnival Miami/Calle Ocho, an annual event that has received both national and international recognition. The carnival is organized by the Kiwanis Club of Little Havana and sponsored by other important local organizations which include *The Miami Herald/El Nuevo Herald*, WQBA La Cubanísima, WAQI, Radio Mambí, WLTV Channel 23, WSCV Channel 51, South East Bank, and Republic National Bank. The posters show the economic impact of Cubans in the United States as recognized by sponsors such as Adolph Coors Company, Anheuser Busch, Stroh Brewery, Miller Brewing Company, Old Milwaukee Beer, Van Munchen and Company, Pepsi Cola, Dole Fruit and Cream Bars, Eastern Airlines, Proctor and Gamble, R.J. Reynolds Tobacco Company, Bell South Advertising and Publishing, and Sunbelt Sales Promotion Line, to name a few.

Items included in the collection are limited to posters

produced by Cubans or Cuban-Americans in exile and posters produced by non-Cuban artists that relate to a Cuban topic or theme. They have been printed either by individuals or associations. The posters in the collection range in size from 14x11 cm. to 92x122 cm.

The posters included in this bibliography are held in the Archives and Special Collections Department of the University of Miami Library, in Coral Gables, Florida. They are available for room use only to anyone who desires to do research using this collection.

Arrangement

The posters are listed in alphabetical order by title and are numbered sequentially. Exceptions to the strict alphabetical listing are the multiple posters under the titles "Carnaval Miami," "Hispanic Heritage Festival," and "Paella," which are grouped together in chronological order.

Each entry contains description of the poster that includes title, text (in the original language of the poster), artist's name as it appears on the poster (or a more complete name, if found), place of publication, publisher, year of publication, color, size, and call number within the Cuban Exile Poster Collection.

Indexes

The Subject index follows Library of Congress's *Subject Headings* as closely as possible. Assigned headings are derived either from the title or the theme of the poster. Names of associations, institutions, clubs, and so forth are indexed under their established proper names; for example, posters treating Las Máscaras theater are cited under "Patronato del Teatro Las Máscaras;" SIBI is found under "Centro Cultural SIBI (Miami, Florida)."

The alphabetically-arranged Artist Index includes the name of the artist as it appears on the poster unless a more complete name has been identified. In both indexes, references are to the entry numbers of the citations.

BIBLIOGRAPHY

1. A Cuba, con el fusil en la mano. Abdala. [Artist] : Luis
    Fernández-Puente. [Miami, Fla., 1970?]
    Hand colored; 28 x 21.5 cm.
    C87-2-PO-2

2. A veces es necesario y forzoso que un hombre muera por un
    pueblo pero jamás ha de morir todo un pueblo por un hombre
    solo. Pedro Luis Boitel... 20,000 ejecuciones... Un millón
    de cubanos han huído del país... Washington D.C.:
    Georgetown University Cuban Students Association, 1973.
    Color; 63.5 x 48.3 cm.
    C-P683D54:W3P45C8/f-1 no. 1

3. Abdala, XI Congreso Nacional, julio 31-agosto 2, clausura
    pública--Bayfront Park Auditorium, domingo 2 de agosto,
    2:00 p.m. [Artist: David Medina. Miami, Fla, 1980].
    B&w; 43 x 28 cm.
    C87-2-PO-25

4. Addimu, ofrenda a los orichas. Oba Ecún. La obra que
    completa la trilogía de: Ita, mitología de la religión
    Yoruba. Oricha, mitología de la religión Yoruba.
    Editorial SIBI. [Artist:] Talamas. [Miami, Fla.] :
    Editorial S.I.B.I. [n.d.]
    Color; 44.0 x 28.5 cm.
    C-P683F44:M5F613/f-1 no. 6

5. Adventure in Music '75. Mario Lanz Salas. Artistic
    director: Renee Pérez... Sunday, April 6, Café Teatro
    Versailles Hotel. [Miami, Fla,] : Forum Productions, 1975.
    B&w;26.4 x 39.4 cm.
    C-P683F44:M5C8M813/f-1 no. 7

6. Agosto 2-5, Congreso Nacional 1973 Abdala III.
    [Commemorative poster. Limited edition. Designed by Luis
    Fernández-Puente. Miami, Fla., 1973?]
    Color; 87 x 58 cm.
    C87-2-PO-7

7. Agrupación Abdala, acto patriótico cubano en conmemoración
    del Grito de Baire... sábado, febrero 27, 7 p.m. Grito de
    Independencia. [Gainesville, Fla., 1972].
    Color; 35 x 22 cm.
    C87-2-PO-3

8. Agrupación Abdala XI Congreso Internacional. Hacia la
    victoria interna con el apoyo externo. Julio 30-Agosto 2,
    1981. [Artist] : David Medina. Autographed. Miami,
    Fla., 1981.
    Color; 76.4 x 55.0 cm.
    C87-2-PO-30

9. Ahora su firma cobrará una dimensión parcial. "Recordar es
    volver a vivir"... Southeast Banks. En bancos...lo máximo.
    [Miami, Fla., n.d.]
    Color; 56.0 x 35.5 cm.
    C-P683F44:M5B8B3/f-1 no. 1

10. Al carnaval con Skoal Bandits. Gane, win 1989 Grand Prix.
    Aviso: este producto no es una alternativa segura a los
    cigarillos. [Artist] : Carreño [Miami, Fla.], 1989.
    Color; 50.9 x 40.6 cm.
    C-P683F44:M5F4C3/f-6 no. 55

11. Alberto Morgan y A-1 Production presentan Ochún Obbayeye.
    Obra musical afrocubana... Promotor y manager: Alberto P.
    González y David C. Reiner. Dade County Auditorium.
    [Miami, Fla., n.d.]
    B&w; 22.3 x 17.0 cm.
    C-P683F44:M5F613/f-1 no. 1

12. Alejandro Obregón recent paintings... October 11-November
    14, 1982. Metropolitan Museum of Art Center... January 10-
    February 14, 1985. Museum of Modern Art of Latin America.
    Organization of American States... [New York]: Arco-Laser,
    [n.d.]
    Color; 68.0 x 49.4 cm.
    C-P683F44:C67C8A713/f-1 no. 1

13. Alfredo Rolando Ortiz. From reviews: "A unique musical
    experience"... California, [199-?]
    Color; 28.5 x 44.4 cm.

14. All Lizt piano recital, Teresa Escandón. Saturday October
    17, 1987, 8:00 p.m. Gusman Hall... Presented by The Cuban
    Museum of Art and Culture in collaboration with the
    University of Miami School of Music, and The Palm Beach
    Invitational International Piano Competition... Photo: Luis
    Castañeda. [Miami, Fla.] : Precision Printing, 1987.
    B&w; 35.5 x 21.6 cm.
    C-P683F44:M5C8C613/f-3 no. 24

15. America wake up! Communism is only 90 miles away. Fidel
    Castro, Moscow's puppet, is subverting our Western
    Hemisphere... Stand up! The time is now! Give our Cuban
    freedom fighters "support" to fight Castro and regain our

8. Agrupación Abdala XI Congreso Internacional.
Artist: David Medina. Miami, Fla., 1981.

country to democracy. R. Caldevilla. [Miami, Fla.], 1981.
Color; 59.5 x 43.2 cm.
C-P683F44:M5A513/f-1 no. 4

16. America wake-up. Fidel Castro is a threat to the peace of
the Western Hemisphere! Castro's Cuba is an arsenal of
Soviet weaponry and ground troops. Their main objective is
to destabilize western democracies through terror and
violence. They will succeed unless Castro is destroyed.
Support all anti-Castro organizations. [Miami, Fla., 1980?]
Color; 28.2 x 22.0 cm.
C-P683F44:M5A513/f-1 no. 3

17. America wake up! This is Castro's Cuba, the "First Free
Territory of the Americas" and the major threat to peace in
the Western Hemisphere. Castro's Cuba exports subversion,
terrorism, narcotics. Wake up, America! Tomorrow may be
too late!... [Miami, Fla., 1986?]
Color; 29.0 x 44.3 cm.
C-P683F44:M5A513/f-1 no. 1

18. La Amistad de tres mujeres en un testimonio único, Rosario
Hiriart. Cartas a Lydia Cabrera (correspondencia inédita
de Gabriela Mistral y Teresa de la Parra). [Artist]:
Gastón Cirmeuge. Torremozas, [1988].
Color; 43.0 x 32.0 cm.
C-P683F44:M5F613C3/f-1 no. 2

19. Amnistía general para los presos políticos cubanos en
cárceles de U.S.A. Lino González. Himno Nacional de
Cuba... Espartaco. [Miami, Fla., 197-?]
B&w; 35.5 x 21.6 cm.
C-P681:C7/f-1 no. 1

20. Año Santo. Renovación espiritual. La Arquidiócesis de
Miami celebra su vigésimo aniversario. [Miami, Fla.,
1973].
Color; 61.5 x 45.8 cm.
C-P683F44:M5R5C3V4/f-1 no. 1

21. Añorada Cuba. Febrero 25, 2:00 pm. Dade County
Auditorium... *Diario Las Américas*, Sazón Goya, WLTV 23, "S"
printing, Super Q, W-QBA, *Reader's Digest Selecciones*.
[Miami, 198-?]
Color; 41.7 x 60.3 cm.
C-P683F44:M5S413A5/f-1 no. 3

22. Las Antiguas Alumnas del Apostolado y la Juventud de San
Isidro presentan "Bajo mi Cielo Tropical". Gran Festival
Musical Folklórico Antillano. Noviembre 2 de 1985... Dade
County Auditorium... 95 jóvenes. Bella música... A

beneficio de las misiones apostolinas en América. [Miami,
Fla.], 1985.
Color; 23.8 x 21.5 cm.
C-P683F44:M5F4M813/f-1 no. 3

23. Arlequín Sala Teatro. Chabela Taquechel presenta una
dirección de Mario Martín... Presentación en Miami de Juan
Troya en Un Sombrero lleno de lluvia de Michael V. Gazzo.
Puede la droga destruir un matrimonio? Carlos Bermúdez,
Cary Roque, Klaudio Morgan. Funciones: viernes y sábados 9
p.m. domingos 5 y 9 p.m... [Miami, Fla., n.d.]
B&w; 43.2 x 27.3 cm.
C-P683F44:M5T513S3/f-1 no. 2

24. Arte en el Presidio Político Cubano, Exclub, Miami, julio
1987, Museo Cubano de Arte y Cultura. Diseñado por:
Salvador E. Subirá. [Miami, Fla.] 1987.
Color; 56.1 x 81.5 cm.
C-P683F44:M5M813M8/f-1 no. 5

25. Artista exclusivo CLM, Janine. [Miami, Fla., n.d.]
Color; 46.0 x 32.0 cm.
C-P683F44:M5C8C613/f-2 no. 16

26. Arts Development Center presenta a "La mejor intérprete de
la música cubana." Zenaida Manfugás... Noviembre 15,
domingo 3:00 p.m. Miami Senior High Auditorium...
Patrocinado por RHC Cadena Azul [and] Arts Development
Center. [Miami, Fla., n.d.]
B&w; 42.8 x 28.0 cm.
C-P683F44:M5C8C613/f-3 no. 22

27. Arts Development Center y Coors Beer presentan: Miami High
Auditorium... abril 23, sábado 8:00 p.m. 24, domingo 3:00
p.m. El estreno en Miami de la grandiosa zarzuela cubana:
Amalia Batista del mtro. Rodrigo Prats. [Artist] :
Cantelli. [Miami, Fla., n.d.]
Color; 43.0 x 35.5 cm.
C-P683F44:M5C8Z313/f-1 no. 5

28. Así fué la Nochebuena en el exilio. Así fué la Nochebuena
en Cuba. Esa mesa que hay en Cuba hay que llenarla el año
que viene... [Artist] : Gadelay. Miami : Nacionalismo
Realista, [n.d.]
B&w; 57.3 x 22.3 cm.
C-P683F44:M5L45C8/f-1 no. 3

29. The Association of Hispanic Arts Inc. celebrating a new
decade: 80's. At Symphony Space. March 16th, 1980, 2
p.m.-6 p.m... The AHA/CETA Artist Project is made possible
by the Department of Cultural Affairs [et al]. This

ARTE EN EL PRESIDIO POLITICO CUBANO

EXCLUB

MIAMI, JULIO/1987

MUSEO CUBANO DE ARTE Y CULTURA

24.   Arte en el Presidio Político Cubano.   Designed by Salvador
E. Subirá.   Miami, Fla., 1987.

performance is made possible with public funds of the New York State Council on the Arts. Design: Malmgren Restrepo. New York, [1980].
Color; 56.2 x 35.5 cm.
C-P683N74:N4A76/f-1 no. 2

30.   BH/2 Exhibition in three locations, October 2-23, 1981. Fernando García. [Miami, Fla.], 1981.
Color; 46.0 x 45.5 cm.
C-P683F44:M5C8A713/f-1 no. 1

31.   Bacardí Art Gallery. A community service to South Florida supported by Bacardí Imports Inc. since 1963. American Prints: From colonial times to 1950. Edward Hopper (1882-1967), Night Shadows, 1921, 11 May-22 June. [Miami, Fla.], 1984.
B&w; 56.0 x 43.0 cm.
C-P683F44:M5C8A7B3/f-1 no. 5

32.   Bacardí Art Gallery... Contemporary Hispanic Art. Works by artists from Spain and Hispanic America under the auspices of the Christopher Columbus Quicentenary Jubilee Commission, 23 October through 5 December, 1986. Antonio Saura, "Galería de América." E.A. IV/XV, lithograph, 65 x 50 cm. Photography by Roland I. Unruh. Miami : Modern Printing & Lithographing, Inc., [1986].
Color; 43.0 x 64.8 cm.
C-P683F44:M5C8A7B3/f-1 no. 1

33.   Bacardí Art Gallery... Fifth Annual Student Exhibition, works by students from Dade County Public Schools participating in the Museum Education Program... 17 July-28 August 1987... Designed by Juan Espinosa/Graphic Design. Consultant: Daniel J. Ramírez. Photography by Roland I. Unruh. Miami, Fla.: International Press of Miami, Inc., 1987.
Color; 51.5 x 30.5 cm.
C-P683F44:M5C8A7B3/f-2 no. 14

34.   Bacardí Art Gallery... Romare Bearden: drawing, collage, printing & watercolor. In celebration of Black History Month, February, 1985. On the cover: Mississippi Monday, multiple collage. Designed by Juan Espinosa. Miami: Central Press, [1985].
Color; 56.0 x 43.1 cm.
C-P683F44:M5C8A7B3/f-1 no. 3

35.   Bacardí Art Gallery... Watercolors, etchings and posters by Jean Michel Folon, 4-30 January 1985. Pensees, watercolor, 1982. Designed by Juan Espinosa. Miami : Central Press, 1985.

Color; 56.0 x 35.5 cm.
C-P683F44:M5C8A7B3/f-1 no. 4

36. Bacardí Art Gallery presents Arte de Guatemala, 3 June
through 1 July, 1983. The Bacardí Art Gallery is a gallery
not-for-profit supported as a community service by Bacardí
Imports, Inc. [Artist] : Carlos Mérida. [Miami, Fla.],
1983.
Color; 55.2 x 27.0 cm.
C-P683F44:M5C8A7B3/f-1 no. 9

37. Bacardí Art Gallery presents Daniel Serra-Badué. A
retrospective survey of paintings and lithographs, 6 May
through 31 May 1983. The Bacardí Art Gallery is a gallery
not-for-profit supported as a community service by Bacardí
Imports, Inc. Carlos Mérida. [Miami, Fla.], 1983.
Color; 44.6 x 38.0 cm.
C-P683F44:M5C8A7B3/f-1 no. 10

38. Bacardí Art Gallery 20th Anniversary Season, 1983/84.
Frederick Eversley, untitled, 1983, red spiral arch. Recent
Sculpture, 3 February through 16 March, [Miami, Fla.],
1984.
Color; 56.0 x 35.7 cm.
C-P683F44:M5C8A7B3/f-1 no. 6

39. Bacardí Art Gallery 20th Anniversary Season 1963/1983.
Bacardí Art Gallery presents Our Spanish Heritage a
selection from the collections at Vizcaya Museum... [Miami,
Fla.], 1983.
Color; 63.5 x 47.0 cm.
C-P683F44:M5C8A7B3/f-1 no. 8

40. Bacardí Art Gallery 20th Anniversary Season, 1963/1983.
Beyond the Figure, urban sculpture. Bacardí Plaza. Michael
Flick, Fernando García, Peter Kuentzel, Robert Huff, Elliot
Miller, Robert Thiele, Jean Ward, William Ward... [Miami,
Fla., 1983].
Color; 56.0 x 47.0 cm.
C-P683F44:M5C8A7B3/f-1 no. 7

41. Bacardi rum mixes with everything. Except driving. Rum 80
proof. All trademarks shown herein are registered. Miami,
FL : Bacardi Imports, Inc., c. 1982.
Color; 70.8 x 53.5 cm.
C-P683F44:M5B813B3/f-1 no. 1

42. Bajo mi cielo tropical. Las ex-alumnas del Apostolado y la
Juventud de San Isidro presentan "Bajo mi cielo tropical",
Dade County Auditorium.. Fecha: Nov. 2, 1985. [Miami,
Fla.], 1985.

Color; 23.8 x 21.5 cm.
C-P683F44:M5F4M813/f-1 no. 2

43. Ballet Concerto Co., Hispanic-American Lyric Theatre
    presents great scenes from Guiditta, Franz Lehár. Janet
    Rodríguez, Giselle Elgarresta, Jorge Mattox, Paul Gibson.
    June 1 & 2, 8 P.M. [Miami, Fla., n.d.]
    Color; 35.4 x 21.7
    C-P683F44:M5C8B313/f-2 no. 13

44. Ballet Concerto Co. presents A gala performance with
    Eleanor D'Antuono & Danilo Radojevic. Courtesy of American
    Ballet Theatre in Paquita... Also premiere in Miami:
    Capriccio Espagnol... Full corps de ballet. Directed by:
    Sonia Díaz, Martha del Pino, Eduardo Recalt, Ana María,...
    Costume designer: Antonio... Florida Philharmonic
    conductor: Alfredo Munar. Dade County Auditorium, 8:15 p.m.
    [Miami, Fla., n.d.]
    Color; 54.5 x 34.4 cm.
    C-P683F44:M5C8B313/f-1 no. 8

45. Ballet Concerto Co. presents "Bayaderka" premiere in Miami.
    Also Cain and Abel. Adagio, Don Quixote, Black Swan...
    Directed by: Sonia Díaz, Martha del Pino, Eduardo Recalt.
    Full orchestra conductor: Paul Csonka... Dade County
    Auditorium, May 12, Saturday, 8:30 . [Miami, Fla., n.d.]
    Color; 35.5 x 21.7 cm.
    C-P683F44:M5C8B313/f-1 no. 3

46. Ballet Concerto Co. presents Don Quixote, Yerma, Giselle,
    with Valentina and Leonid Koslovs, former stars of the
    Bolshoi Ballet. Guest artist Miguel de Grandy II, Mariana
    Alvarez, Addy Castellanos, Susie García, Carlos González,
    Sissi Infante. Directed by Sonia Díaz, Martha del Pino,
    Eduardo Recalt. Costume designer: Antonio... Full
    orchestra conductor: Alfredo Munar. Dade County
    Auditorium, March 28, 8:15 p.m., Friday. [Miami, Fla.,
    n.d.]
    Color; 51.5 x 39.5 cm.
    C-P683F44:M5C8B313/f-1 no. 9

47. Ballet Concerto Co. presents Giselle, full length with
    Natalia Makarova, Ivan Nagy. Miguel Campanería, Hilda
    Reverté [et al]. Directed by Sonia Díaz, Marta del Pino,
    Eduardo Recalt... Costume designer: Antonio. Full
    orchestra conductor: Paul Csonka... May 18, Dade County
    Auditorium, 8:15 p.m. [Miami, Fla., n.d.]
    Color; 54.5 x 34.4 cm.
    C-P683F44:M5C8B313/f-1 no. 10

48. Ballet Concerto Co. presents La Fille Mal Gardeé, Opus 22,

Don Quixote... Full orchestra conductor: Alfredo Munar.
Directed by: Sonia Díaz, Martha del Pino, Eduardo Recalt.
Costume designs by: Antonio...Miami Beach Theatre of the
Performing Arts, Friday, April 30, 1976, 8:15 p.m. [Miami,
Fla.], 1976.
Color; 28.7 x 18.2 cm.
C-P683F44:M5C8B313/f-1 no. 5

49. Ballet Concerto Co. presents Les Sylphides, Don Quixote,
Goyescas, pas de trois, Spring Waters. Natalia Makarova,
Ivan Nagy [et al]. Directed by Sonia Díaz, Martha del Pino,
Eduardo Recalt. Costume design: Antonio... Conductor:
Alberto Fajardo. December 18, 8:15 p.m. Dade County
Auditorium. [Miami, Fla., n.d.]
Color; 35.5 x 19.9 cm.
C-P683F44:M5C8B313/f-1 no. 6

50. Ballet Concerto Co. presents Swan Lake, Romeo, Trois
Chansons, Polyphony. Guest artist: Mariana Alvarez, Carlos
González, Addy Castellanos, Sissi Infante [et al].
Directed by Sonia Díaz, Martha del Pino, Eduardo Recalt.
Costume designer: Antonio... Conductor: Alfredo Munar.
Dade County Auditorium, November 8, 1980. [Miami, Fla.],
1980.
Color; 55.2 x 43.0 cm.
C-P683F44:M5C8B313/f-2 no. 11

51. Ballet Concerto Co. sponsored by *Diario las Américas*
presents afternoon at the ballet with the world premiere.
Arnaldo Silva's Lola premiere. Lorenzo Monreal's Emotions
I-II-III premiere. Eduardo Recalt's Yerma premiere. General
directors: Sonia Díaz, Martha del Pino, Eduardo Recalt.
With Addy Castellanos, Sissi Infante [et al]. Dade County
Auditorium. Sunday, February 4, 1979. [Miami, Fla.], 1979.
B&w; 61.0 x 45.5 cm.
C-P683F44:M5C8B313/f-1 no. 4

52. Ballet Vivian Tobío presents Tarzán. World premier
spectacular production. July 27, 1991. Dade County
Auditorium... Artistic director Vivian Tobío. Special
appearancee by the three time ACCA award winners David
Nuñez and Lilian Vigo. [Miami, Fla.], 1991.
Color; 76.3 x 50.8 cm.
C-P683F44:M5C8B313/f-2 no. 15

53. Beatrice Indy Challenge. Tamiami Park, Miami, Florida.
November 9, 1985. [Miami, Fla.?], 1985.
Color; 96.0 x 61.0 cm.
C-P683F44:M5I5/f-1 no. 1

54. El Becerro de oro, Joaquín L. Luaces, comedia costumbrista

cubana del siglo XIX presentada por el Koubek Memorial
Center, escuela de estudios continuados de la Universidad
de Miami como homenaje a la Semana de la Herencia
Hispánica. Dirección y dramaturgia: A. Naser... Diseño y
dibujo: M. de la Portilla. [Miami, Fla., 1983].
B&w; 39.6 x 26.5 cm.
C-P683F44:M5T613/f-1 no. 2

55. Bicentenario del natalicio del Padre Félix Varela, 20 de
noviembre 1788-20 de noviembre 1988. Unete a los actos de
honor al precursor de la independencia de Cuba. Conoce y
divulga la vida y obra del primer exiliado cubano. Asiste:
peregrinación a San Agustín, conferencia en el Koubek
Center... Comité del Bicentenario de Félix Varela... Miami,
Fla., [1988].
B&w; 35.0 x 22.2 cm.
C-P683F44:M5R5C313V3/f-1 no. 1

56. Bienvenidos. Carnival Miami Little Havana, U.S.A. Mazola
Corn Oil. San Antonio, Texas : Sunbelt Sales Promotion
Line, 1987.
Color; 71.2 x 55.7 cm.
C-P683F44:M5F4C3/f-4 no. 33

57. Boniato, Cuba '75... [Artist: Luis Fernández-Puente].
Elizabeth, NJ, [1975].
Color; 56 x 42 cm.
C87-2-PO-11

58. Budweiser, Busch, Budlight. 1984 Carnival Miami, Little
Havana, U.S.A. Calle Ocho, March 4, 1984. Carnival night,
March 10, 1984. Celia Cruz... La tremenda Budweiser Salsa
Band. Paseo route: Flagler Street to S.W. 21 Ave. to S.W.
1st St. to S.W. 14th Ave... [Miami, Fla.], 1984.
Color; 29.0 x 21.8 cm.
C-P683F44:M5F4C3/f-3 no. 25

59. Budweiser Grand Prix of Miami. Feb. 25. 26. 1984.
Amoroso. [Miami, Fla.] : Distributed by Miami Poster Co.,
1984.
Color; 71.2 x 53.5 cm.
C-P683F44:M5G7/f-1 no. 2

60. Budweiser. Grand Prix of Miami. [Official Poster. Miami,
Fla., n.d.]
Color; 87.6 x 50.8 cm.
C-P683F44:M5G7/f-1 no. 3

61. Budweiser Grand Prix of Miami. Sunday, February 27.
Qualifying day - Saturday February 26. Two full days of
racing action on the streets of downtown Miami... Official

sponsors of the Budweiser Grand Prix of Miami: Coca Cola,
Canon Cameras, Herma Watches... St Louis, MO : Bush
Creative Services Corporation, 1983.
Color; 73.7 x 43.2 cm.
C-P683F44:M5G7/f-1 no. 1

62. Budweiser, king of beers. 1979 Hispanic Heritage Week.
Folkloric festival. S.W. Eight Street, October 14.
[Miami, Fla.], 1979.
Color; 24.5 x 92.0 cm.
C-P683F44:M5F4H5/f-1 no. 2

63. Budweiser, king of beers presenta: Calle Ocho 1983. Celia
Cruz con la Sonora Matancera. Wilfrido Vargas. Orquesta
Sevilla Biltmore, Conjunto Universal. Marzo 6, domingo.
[St. Louis, Mo.] : Anheuser-Busch, Inc. [1984].
Color; 61.0 x 45.5 cm.
C-P683F44:M5F4C3/f-1 no. 1

64. Budweiser, Michelob se unen a ustedes en Carnaval Miami,
Little Havana, U.S.A. '86 Calle Ocho Open House. Tito
Puente, Celia Cruz, Hansel & Raúl, Carlos Oliva y los
Sobrinos del Juez. Paseo, domingo marzo 2. 8k Run, viernes
marzo 7. Calle Ocho Open House, domingo marzo 9... Design &
art work by: Drago. [Miami, Fla.?], 1986.
Color; 61.0 x 43.2 cm.
C-P683F44:M5F4C3/f-2 no. 17

65. Budweiser presents Calle Ocho '89. Celia Cruz "La reina de
la salsa"... 12 de marzo 1989 en la 23 Ave. y la calle 8.
1984 [Artist] : T. Britt 84. St. Louis, Mo.: Anheuser
Busch Inc., 1984.
Color; 87.0 x 55.5 cm.
C-P683F44:M5F4C3/f-6 no. 59

66. Budweiser presents domingo, 11 de marzo ¡La esquina del
sabor! en la Calle Ocho y la Avenida 23 en los terrenos de
Rainbow Buick: Celia Cruz, El Gran Combo, Roberto Torres,
Orquesta Inmensidad, Johnny Ventura, Luis Enrique, El
Equipo, Conjunto de Aruba. [Artist]: T. Britt. St Louis,
Mo.: Anheuser-Busch Inc., 1984.
Color; 87.5 x 56.0 cm.
C-P683F44:M5F4C3/f-7 no. 67

67. CBA Productions, Néstor Molina, Jeffrey Lane, y Orlando
Rossardi presentan Pilar Arenas, Manolo Villaverde,
Griselda Noguera en La Reina enamorada... Dirección: Maria
Julia Casanova. Teatro de Bellas Artes. [Miami, Fla.,
n.d.]
Sepia; 43.0 x 27.9 cm.
C-P683F44:M5T513T42/f-1 no. 3

68. California Institute of the Arts. The Cuban poster, a full
    circle. Cuban poster exhibition April 21-23 1987, 9 a.m.
    until 8 p.m. Mezzanine Gallery... [Valencia, Ca.] :
    California Institute of the Arts, 1987.
    Color; 62.3 x 45.4 cm.
    C-P683C34:V3C8A713/f-1 no. 1

69. Calle Ocho. Budweiser y los Kiwanis of Little Havana
    presentan Celia Cruz en concierto. Budweiser Light. Hansel,
    Raúl y Charanga, Conjunto Impacto, Conjunto Universal,
    Mónica y su Grupo Clouds, marzo 14. St. Louis, Missouri :
    Anheuser Busch, Inc., 1982.
    Color; 68.5 x 48.3 cm.
    C-P683F44:M5F4C3/f-2 no. 11

70. Calle Ocho, Carnaval. Design by Marcelo Rossetti. Miami,
    Florida: Dole Fruit 'N Juice, Marzo 1985.
    Color; 53.0 x 41.0 cm.
    C-P683F44:M5F4C3/f-3 no. 27

71. Calle Ocho map. Mar. 15th, 1987. Anniversary.
    [Miami, Fla.], 1987.
    Color; 61.0 x 90.0 cm.
    C-P683F44:M5F4C3/f-5 no. 47

72. Calle Ocho 1985 party. Las verdaderas páginas amarillas...
    para usted! [Miami, Fla.] : Bell South Advertising &
    Publishing, 1985.
    Color; 76.5 x 61.0 cm.
    C-P683F44:M5F4C3/f-4 no. 32

73. Calle Ocho: Open House Eight, an invitation to S.W. 8th
    St., March 8, 1981. Miami, Florida. Compliments of *The
    Miami Herald/El Miami Herald*. [Designed by]: Michele León
    Fox. Miami: Kiwanis of Little Havana, 1981.
    Color; 63.5 x 48.4 cm.
    C-P683F44:M5F4C3/f-1 no. 9

74. Calle Ocho: Open House Eight, an invitation to S.W. 8th St,
    March 11, 1979. Miami, Florida. [Designed by] Michelle
    León Fox. [Miami, Fla.] : Kiwanis of Little Havana, 1979.
    Color; 61.5 x 48.5 cm.
    C-P683F44:M5F4C3/f-1 no. 5

75. Calle Ocho: Open House Eight, an invitation to S.W. 8th St,
    March 9, 1980. Miami, Florida. [Designed by:] Michelle
    León Fox. [Miami, Fla.] : Kiwanis Club of Little Havana,
    [1980].
    Color; 61.5 x 48.5 cm.
    C-P683F44:M5F4C3/f-1 no. 6

76.   Calle Ocho Open House, March 10, 1985. Calle Ocho program.
[Map with location of events]. Shuttle service... [Miami,
Fla.], 1985.
Color; 44.3 x 58.5 cm.
C-P683F44:M5F4C3/f-4 no. 31

77.   Calle Ocho salutes the U.S.A. [Miami, Fla., n.d.]
Color; 58.5 x 89.3 cm.
C-P683F44:M5F4C3/f-5 no. 46

78.   Calle Ocho. Seven Up invites you to Calle Ocho Open House
Eight, Sunday, March 9, 1:00 p.m. Seven Up los invita...
[Designed by]: J. Dickinson. [Miami, Fla., 1983?]
Color; 91.5 x 61.0 cm.
C-P683F44:M5F4C3/f-3 no. 21

79.   Calle Ocho. Sunday, March 9, 1986, 1:00 p.m. to 8:00 p.m.
SW 8 St. from 6 Ave. to 27 Ave. Sponsored by Kiwanis Club
of Little Havana & *The Miami Herald*. Carnival Miami,
Little Havana U.S.A. Poster designed by Teresita García.
[Miami, Fla.], 1986.
Color; 63.5 x 47.8 cm.
C-P683F44:M5F4C3/f-2 no. 18

80.   Camila es Cuba, Camila es risa, pasión, alegría, es el
toque de un tambor afro-cubano. Camila es Changó, en un
solar habanero, en tiempos de la revolución. Círculo CEM
presenta Santa Camila de la Habana Vieja. Dirección y
adaptación: Eduardo Corbe... Agosto 3-septiembre 9...
Teatro América. [Miami, Fla., n.d.]
Color; 43.0 x 27.8 cm.
C-P683F44:M5T513T4/f-1 no. 1

81.   Cañaveral. The University of Miami presents a concert of
traditional Hispanic-American music. Place: Koubek
Memorial Center. Date: Friday, October 10, 1986. Time:
8:00 p.m. [Miami, Fla., 1986].
B&w; 35.5 x 31.6 cm.
C-P683F44:M5U55K6P7/f-1 no. 2

82.   Capacidad y experencia al servicio de la Pequeña Habana.
Vote #169. Morse, representante - Distrito 113. [Miami,
Fla., n.d.]
Color; 58.8 x 33.4 cm.
C-P683F44:M5P513H68/f-1 no. 2

83.   Caribank presenta Grupo Cañaveral, recital de canciones
hispanoamericanas, programa "Audiciones" Universidad de
Miami. Lugar: Koubek Memorial Center... Fecha: viernes, 15
de mayo de 1987. Hora: 8:00 P.M... [Miami, Fla.], 1987.
Color; 35.5 x 21.6 cm.

C-P683F44:M5U55K6P7/f-1 no. 3

84. Caridad del Cobre. Ricardo Pedreguera's sketch that
originated the mural painted in the heart of the Latin
Quarter in Little Havana U.S.A. City of Miami: Little
Havana Development Authority. Department of Trade and
Commerce, 1975.
Color; 66.2 x 51.0 cm.
C-P683F44:M5R4P41308/f-1 no. 4

85. Carlos Pérez Congreso. "Carlos Pérez... merece ser el
próximo miembro del Congreso de los Estados Unidos..." Lt.
Col. Oliver North, Miami - junio 29, 1989. Pérez for
Congress Committee.. Pd. Pol. Adv./ Republican. [Miami,
Fla., 1989].
Color; 43.2 x 28.0 cm.
C-P683F44:M5P513H69/f-1 no. 3

86. Carlos Pérez, congressman... continúe la tradición. Paid
for by Carlos Pérez for Congress Campaign Committee.
[Miami, Fla., 1989].
Color; 35.5 x 56.6 cm.
C-P683F44:M5P513H69/f-1 no. 4

87. Carnaval 78. Omni International, January 7, 1978.
Miami, Fla.: Eastern Airlines, 1978.
Color; 60.0 x 42.5 cm.
C-P683F44:M5F4C3/f-1 no. 4

88. Carnaval Miami, Calle Ocho Open House. USA TH(Top Hits)-
Rodven, le pone música al carnaval con sus artistas
participantes!... Radio Mambí/WRHC Cadena Azul, Unión
Radio, Hit T.V. [et al]. Art work & design by: Drago,
[Miami, Fla., 198-?]
Color; 59.5 x 41.5 cm.
C-P683F44:M5F4C3/f-4 no. 38

89. Carnaval Miami '84. Sunday, March 4, Calle Ocho Open House.
Saturday, March 10, Carnaval Night, Orange Bowl Stadium.
Sunday, March 11, Winston Paseo. Winston lo tiene todo.
Winston, R.I.: Reynolds Tobacco Co., 1984.
Color; 53.5 x 40.5 cm.
C-P683F44:M5F4C3/f-3 no. 24

90. Carnaval Miami, Little Havana U.S.A. Marzo 3 a marzo 11,
1984. [Designed by]: Aldo Amador. Golden, Colorado : Adolph
Coors Company, 1984.
Color; 56.7 x 40.7 cm.
C-P683F44:M5F4C3/f-3 no. 23

91. Carnaval Miami 1986. Little Havana U.S.A. Tome con cuidado.

97. Carnaval Miami 90, Calle Ocho. Miami, Fla., 1990.

Tom González, cubano, premiado como ilustrador y diseñador, ha sido comisionado por la compañía Adolph Coors para capturar con estilo la esencia del Carnaval Miami. Golden, Colorado : Adolph Coors Company, 1986.
Color; 66.0 x 48.0 cm.
C-P683F44:M5F4C3/f-2 no. 16

92. Carnival Miami '88. Kiwanis of Little Havana Calle Ocho Open House. Souvenir poster courtesy of *The Miami Herald,* Southeast Bank, *el Nuevo Herald*. [Miami, Fla.], 1988.
Color; 61.2 x 42.0 cm.
C-P683F44:M5F4C3/f-5 no. 49

93. Carnival Miami '88. Souvenir poster courtesy of *The Miami Herald*, Southeast Bank, *El Nuevo Herald*. Carnival Miami, Little Havana U.S.A., Kiwanis of Little Havana, Calle Ocho Open House. [Miami, Fla.], 1988.
Color; 61.0 x 42.0 cm.
C-P683F44:M5F4C3/f-7 no. 63

94. Carnaval Miami, Little Havana U.S.A. Para la sed de la nueva generación. Calle Ocho, sponsored by Kiwanis of Little Havana. [Artist:] Hierro. Created/produced by Graphic Arts Advertising Studio, West New York, N.J.: 1989.
Color; 82.0 x 54.5 cm.
C-P683F44:M5F4C3/f-6 no. 54

95. Carnival Miami '89. Souvenir poster courtesy of *The Miami Herald*, Southeast Bank, *El Nuevo Herald*. [Miami, Fla., 1989].
Color; 61.0 x 45.7 cm.
C-P683F44:M5F4C3/f-6 no. 57

96. Carnival Miami '89. Souvenir poster courtesy of *The Miami Herald*, Southeast Bank, *El Nuevo Herald*. Carnival Miami, Little Havana U.S.A., Kiwanis Club. [Miami, Fla., 1989].
Color; 61.0 x 45.9 cm.
C-P683F44:M5F4C3/f-7 no. 62

97. Carnival Miami 90, Calle Ocho. Kiwanis Club, Little Havana. Souvenir poster courtesy of *The Miami Herald*, Southeast Bank, *El Nuevo Herald*. [Miami, Fla., 1990].
Color; 61.0 x 45.9 cm.
C-P683F44:M5F4C3/f-7 no. 68

98. Celebración de los 30 años en el teatro de la primera actriz cómica Sandra Hayde... Monumental espectáculo cómico-musical con Néstor Cabel y su compañía María Luisa Chorens, Johnny Rojas [et al], lunes 21 de abril 1986... Teatro de Bellas Artes... [Miami, Fla.], 1986.
B&w; 35.5 x 21.5 cm.

C-P683F44:M5H513/f-1 no. 1

99. Celebrando el 3er aniversario, Teatro Las Máscaras
presenta: La más tierna, humana y divertida comedia de
Alejandro Casona, La tercera palabra... Miami High
Auditorium, sábado 11 de marzo. Dirección: Salvador
Ugarte... Fotos: Marcel. [Miami, Fla., n.d.]
Color; 43.2 x 28.0 cm.
C-P683F44:M5T513M3/f-1 no. 3

100. A Celebration of Women. Reclaiming the past... Rewriting
the future... a bilingual poetry reading, Tuesday, March 22
7:30-8:30 p.m. Ana Rosa Núñez and Gladys Zaldívar,
internationally acclaimed poets will recite from their
published works... Miami-Dade Community College, North
Campus. [Miami, Fla.] : Printed by Ross Printing, 1988.
Color; 51.0 x 33.0 c.m.
C-P683F44:M5C8C713/f-1 no. 2

101. Celebre cristianamente la Navidad. Keep Christ in
Christmas. Cortesía de: Consolidated bank. [Miami, Fla.,
n.d.]
Color; 42.0 x 29.0 cm.
C-P683F44:M5R4C313/f-1 no. 2

102. Celebre cristianamente las Navidades, let us put Christ in
Christmas. Cortesía de Figueredo Chevrolet. [Miami,
Fla.], 1981.
Color; 42.0 x 31.0 cm.
C-P683F44:M5R4C313/f-1 no. 1

103. Celia Cruz y los libros con ritmo de música antillana.
Umberto Valverde. Reina Rumba, Celia Cruz, Bomba Cámara.
Prólogo de: Guillermo Cabrera Infante. Editorial La Oveja
Negra : Bogotá, Caracas, La Paz, Lima, Quito... Bogotá,
[n.d.]
Color; 44.1 x 33.6 cm.
C-P683F44:M5M413B6/f-1 no. 1

104. Cena Martiana, 1989. Actividad patriótica-cultural
homenaje al apóstol de Cuba José Martí. Fecha: Enero 27,
1989. Hora: 8 P.M. Hotel: Centro de Convenciones, Grand
Salón. Condado, Puerto Rico... Homenaje a los ex-presos
políticos cubanos y en apoyo a la rebeldía interna en Cuba.
Comité gestor: Gloria Gil, Enrique Blanco Amigó, José
Casas, [et al]... [San Juan, P.R.], 1989.
Color; 53.4 x 39.0 cm.
C-P633P81:M46H613/f-1 no. 1

105. Cena Pro-fondo por el apoyo externo a la lucha interna con
representantes del Movimiento Polaco Solidaridad. Dia de

la lucha antisoviética, domingo 6 de diciembre, 1981.
[Artist]: David Medina, Limited edition. [Miami, Fla.?] :
Agrupación Abdala, 1981.
Color; 60.5 x 45.4 cm.
C87-2-PO-27

106. Centro Cultural Cubano de Nueva York presenta Semana de la
Reafirmación Cultural Cubana. III Festival de Arte Cubano,
20 al 26 de mayo, 1979, Union City, New Jersey. [New
York?], 1979.
Color; 63.5 x 48.4 cm.
C-P683N74:N4F4F3/f-1 no. 1

107. Centro Cultural Cubano presenta a Omar Torres en Notas de
un trapecista (poemas y canciones para matar un domingo).
Dom. 31 de marzo, 6:00 p.m. Cathedral House, Cathedral
Church of St. John the Divine. New York, [n.d.]
Sepia; 36.5 x 25.8 cm.
C-P683N74:N4C8P613/f-1 no. 1

108. El Centro Cultural SIBI presenta a Claudia Dammert en la
deliciosa comedia, "Diamantes en almíbar." Claudia... toda
una "Show woman"... En el piano bar el destacado cantante
del "Feeling" Bobby Jiménez. Viernes 4 de abril...
[Miami, Fla.] : Bass, [n.d.]
Color; 44.3 x 29.0 cm.
C-P683F44:M5T513S5/f-1 no. 2

109. El Centro Cultural SIBI presenta: René Ariza en todo un
poco y otras cositas, el primero con René, primero de enero
de 1986, 5:00 p.m. René Ariza nació en La Habana, es
poeta... [Miami, Fla.], : 1986.
B&w; 43.0 x 27.9 cm.
C-P683F44:M5C8A713/f-1 no. 3

110. Cerveza Coors FM 92 CMQ les invita a bailar en el Festival
Open House Calle Ocho '83 con el Grupo Tierra, La Charanga
76, La Comparsa Juventud Latina, Los Cumbiamberos de Juan
Pablo, y otras sorpresas! Domingo 16 de marzo. The best of
the Rockies is here! Golden, Colorado : Adolph Coors
Company, 1982.
Color; 89.0 cm in diameter.
C-P683F44:M5F4C3/f-2 no. 13

111. La cerveza Heineken saluda Calle Ocho Open House 1989. La
cita es el 12 de marzo de 1 p.m. a 8 p.m. en calle 8 y 11
Ave. del S.W. Exclusive U.S. Importers Van Munching & Co.
Inc., New York, 1989.
Color; 85.0 x 64.5 cm.
C-P683F44:M5F4C3/f-6 no. 58

112. Cerveza Latina Beer. Esta si que es... ¡La que se ganó el
     ño! [Miami, Fla., 1987?]
     Color; 63.3 x 48.0 cm.
     C-P683F44:M5M413B4/f-1 no. 2

113. Cerveza Michelob. Hanzel y Raúl. St. Louis, Mo.:
     Anheuser-Busch, Inc. [1987].
     Color; 55.5 x 43.2 cm.
     C-P683F44:M5F4C3/f-5 no. 48

114. Cerveza Tecate salutes Calle Ocho, March 15, 1987. Be sure
     to visit the Tecate music site at the corner of 12th Ct. at
     8th St. Featuring: "Familia Mora Arriaga". [Miami, Fla.]
     1987.
     Color; 43.0 x 28.0 cm.
     C-P683F44:M5F4C3/f-5 no. 44

115. Chabela A. Taquechel presenta a Concha Valdés Miranda,
     canta a los enamorados... En concierto... Copacabana
     Supper Club. Lunes 13 de febrero 1984. Animación y
     dirección artística Mario Martín. Actuación especial de
     Carlos Guerra... Tickets... Tropical Federal Savings and
     Loans. [Miami, Fla.] : Twin Printing, 1984.
     B&w; 42.5 x 27.7 cm.
     C-P683F44:M5N513C6/f-1 no. 1

116. CXXIX Aniversario del Natalicio de Jose Marti. XIV
     Aniversario de la Agrupación Abdala. 30 de enero de 1982.
     Koubek Center... Miami, Fl. [Artist: David Medina Ariza].
     Autographed. Miami, Fla., [1982].
     Color; 56.1 x 41.8 cm.
     C87-2-PO-32

117. Cirque Cubain à Paris. Internationale de la Résistance
     Droits de l'Homme-Cuba. Cuba: 10.000.000 habitants,
     1,000,000 exilés, 140,000 prisonniers dont 14.000
     prionniers politiques. Bureau Tiers Monde, Paris.
     [Artist:] Luis Ruiz. Gennevilliers: Les Ateliers FUNAM
     [1987?]
     Color; 64.0 x 45.0 cm.
     C-P623F71:F4C513/f-1 no. 1

118. City of Sweetwater. Vote May 13, 1986. Elija a (elect)
     José A. Rivero para Concejal, for Councilman. Paid Pol.
     Ad./ José A. Rivero. [Miami, Fla.] 1986.
     Color; 38.0 x 25.6 cm.
     C-P683F44:S9P513C64/f-1 no. 1

119. Ciudadano: inscríbete para votar y... ¡Vota para que te
     respeten!... Sábado, 17 de septiembre, 1983, 2:00 a 10:00
     p.m. Radio Alegre, CMQ, WLTV 23, lo nuestro. [Miami,

Fla.] 1983.
Color; 61.0 x 40.5 cm
C-P683F44:M5V613/f-1 no. 1

120.   La Coalición de Mujeres Hispano Americanas. Sexta
        conferencia en español La Mujer Hispana: potencial y
        futuro, sábado 27 de febrero 1988. University of Miami,
        Koubek Center. Designed by Juan Urquiola, [Miami, Fla.] :
        Printed by World Printing, Inc., 1988.
        Color; 53.2 x 40.5 cm.
        C-P683F44:M5C8C713/f-1 no. 1

121.   Cold wave hits Calle Ocho. Featuring Eddie Santiago, el
        ídolo de la salsa... Sunday, March 12, 1989. 1:00 p.m. to
        8:00 pm. S.W. 8th street and 2nd Ave. [Artist:] Tom
        Nachreiner. Miller Genuine Draft. Miller de etiqueta
        negra. Milwaukee, Wis.: Miller Brewing Co. 1989.
        Color; 56.0 x 37.2 cm.
        C-P683F44:M5F4C3/f-6 no. 52

122.   Cold wave hits Calle Ocho. Miller genuine draft.
        Featuring: Hansel y la orquesta Calle Ocho... Sunday, March
        11, 1990, 1:00 p.m.-8:00 p.m. FM 92, salsa y sabor. La
        onda fría, Miller de etiquetta... Milwaukee, Wis.: Miller
        Brewing Co., 1990.
        Color; 55.3 x 37.2 cm.
        C-P683F44:M5F4C3/f-7 no. 64

123.   Colección Martí y los niños por Bibí Arenas... [Limited]
        23/100. Autographed. [Miami, Fla.] : Ediciones Lulú
        [n.d.]
        Color; 66.0 x 51.0 cm.
        C-P683F44:M5A713A7/f-1 no. 1

124.   Con la soga al cuello. [Miami, Fla., n.d.]
        Color; 58.6 x 19.6 cm.
        C-P683F44:M5C2S313/f-1 no. 1

125.   Concierto de gala. Carlos Montané, tenor. Lori Piitz,
        pianista... Miami Senior High School, Sunday, September 13.
        [Miami, Fla., n.d.]
        Color; 57.8 x 42.0 cm.
        C-P683F44:M5C8C613/f-2 no. 17

126.   Concierto inolvidable. Gran homenaje a Julio Gutiérrez...
        "Un evento histórico honrando a una verdadera gloria del
        arte musical cubano." Domingo, mayo 24, 1992. 3:00 p.m...
        [Sponsors] : *Diario Las Américas*, WLTV-Miami, fm 92, Havana
        Club, Olmedo Printing. Dade County Auditorium. [Miami,
        Fla., 1992].
        Color; 43.5 x 56.8 cm.

C-P683F44:M5C8C613/f-4 no. 32

127. Concierto P. Félix Varela. 1788-1988 Bicentenario.
Francisco Muller, piano. Celebrando el nacimiento de un
hombre, de un pueblo, de una música... Vivian García
Saavedra, canto. Nov 12, 8:00 p.m. St Brendan's Parish
Center. [Miami, Fla., 1988].
Color; 43.0 x 28.0 cm.
C-P683F44:M5H513/f-1 no. 2

128. Congreso de Literatura Cubana: homenaje a Enrique Labrador
Ruíz...November 15, 16, 17, 1979... Sponsored by:
Department of Modern Languages, Florida International
University; Department of Foreign Languages, Auburn
University; Department of Conferences & Short Courses,
Florida International University; Student Government
Association, Florida International University. [Miami,
Fla.: FIU], 1979.
Color; 45.7 x 40.6 cm.
C-P683F44:M5R5C313V3/f-1 no. 3

129. Coppacabana Supper Club presenta el fabuloso Dyango. El
huracán del Caribe Iris Chacón, desde oct. 31 (Halloween
party). Despida el año con Celia Cruz, [Miami, Fla., n.d.]
Color; 57.1 x 44.3 cm.
C-P683F44:M5N513C6/f-1 no. 3

130. Coral Gables Branch Library, Miami-Dade Public Library
System. Oct. 6-Nov. 19, 1982. Sculptures and drawings,
Pedro Hernández. Autographed and limited 25/45.
[Miami, Fla.], 1982.
Silkscreen, b&w; 28.5 x 39.1 cm.
C-P683F44:M5A713H4/f-1 no. 1   c.1

131. Coral Gables Branch Library... Pedro Hernández.
Autographed and limited 26/45. [Miami, Fla.], 1982.
Silkscreen, b&w; 28.5 x 39.1 cm.
C-P683F44:M5A713G6/f-1 no. 1   c.2

132. Creation Ballet Company in concert presents Afreketé.
Choreographed by Pedro Pablo Peña, music composed by Mario
Salas-Lanz, set and costume designed by Rolando Moreno.
The Actor's Playhouse Theatre... Sept. 16 & 17, 1989, Sat.
at 8:30 p.m., Sun. at 5:00 p.m. [Miami, Fla.], 1989.
Sepia; 43.2 x 28.0 cm.
C-P683F44:M5C8B313/f-2 no. 14

133. Creation Ballet Company "world premiere" Afreketé, a Cuban
ballet, featuring Mercedes Conde in the title role. Music
composed and performed by: Mario Salas-Lanz. Choreography
by: Pedro Pablo Peña. Set and costume designed by: Rolando

134. 4a Feria Nacional de los Municipios de Cuba
en el Exilio. Artist: Matías. Miami, Fla., 1986.

Moreno. Colony Theatre, Lincoln Rd. at Lenox, Miami Beach. Saturday, January 23, 1988, 8:00 p.m. [Artist]: R. Moreno. [Miami, Fla.], 1987.
Color; 55.6 x 34.8 cm.
C-P683F44:M5C8B313/f-2 no. 12

134. 4a Feria Nacional de los Municipios de Cuba en el Exilio. Abril 10-13, 1986. Flager Dog Track. "Un encuentro con la cultura y las tradiciones de la Patria que no se olvida" Matías, [artist]. 1986. [Miami, Fla.], 1986.
Color; 52.5 x 36.0 cm.
C-P683F44:M5F4M7/f-1 no. 4

135. IV Parada Escolar Martiana. School parade honoring José Martí. Viernes 27 de enero... Bayfront Park, Miami/78. Asoc. de Escuelas Privadas Bilingües. Martin Studio. [Miami, Fla., 1978].
Color; 45.0 x 27.9 cm.
C-P683F44:M5M46P213/f-1 no. 1

136. Cuba canta y baila. El domingo 7 de agosto en el Dade County Auditorium... con la super estrella de este grandioso espectáculo Blanquita Amaro... para nuestros amigos los vacacionistas, un regalo. [Miami, Fla., n.d.]
B&w; 43.0 x 27.9 cm.
C-P683F44:M5C8M813/f-1 no. 3

137. Cuba: captive island for thousands of Cuban political prisoners: freedom, crusade pro-liberation of Cuban political prisoners. [Miami, Fla., n.d.]
B&w; 43.5 x 28.0 cm.
C-P683F44:M5P6613C8/f-1 no. 4

138. Cuba está de luto! Diciembre 7. Este valiente patriota cubano, supo morir y escribir con sangre, la palabra "Independencia", en la manigua redentora...Miami, diciembre de 1964. Cortesía..."Album Azul de Cuba"... el libro que se escribió en el destierro para la libertad de Cuba. A.G. Dulzaides, editor. [Miami, Fla.: Album Azul de Cuba]. 1964.
Color; 43.3 x 28.0 cm.
C-P683F44:M5M513/f-1 no. 1

139. Cuba, hacia la insurrección nacional, décimo congreso internacional. Miami, julio 31-agosto 3, 1980. [Artist]: P. Carreño. Agrupación Abdala. Limited edition [New Jersey, 1980].
Color; 50 x 39 cm.
C87-2-PO-24

140. Cuba in the Seventies. A lecture series at Georgetown

University. Nov. 2 Cuba in the Era of Realpolitik, Luis E.
Aguilar... Nov. 9 Cuban Poetry in Perspective, Poet Eugenio
Florit... Nov. 16 A Pragmatic Stage in Economic Policy,
Carmelo Mesa Lago... Nov. 30 The Soviet American Cuban
Triangle, James The Berge... [Washington, D.C.: Georgetown
Univ., n.d.]
B&w; 43.0 x 28.0 cm.
C-P683D54:W3C68L4G4/f-1 no. 1

141. Cuba 1871, Cuba 1973. Un testimonio. Lugar: St Stephen
Martyr Church y Auditorium... Diciembre 7 de 1973. Misa:
7:30 p.m. Teatro 8:30 p.m. [Washington, D.C.], 1973.
B&w; 28.0 x 43.3 cm.
C-P683D54:W3A3813/f-1 no. 1

142. Cuba te espera! Cita con nuestro destino. Bienvenido
Presidente Ronald Reagan. Oradores: Presidente Ronald
Reagan, Jorge L. Mas Canosa, Embajador Armando Valladares.
Orange Bowl. Miami, Florida. Sábado 28 de abril, 1990.
Hora: 12:00 p.m. The Cuban-American National Foundation.
Entrada gratis. [Miami, Fla.] : The Cuban American
National Foundation, 1990.
Color; 43.5 x 28.0 cm.
C-P683F44:M5F713R3/f-1 no. 1

143. Cuba. The island of Cuba photographed from outer space by
the satellite NOAA at an altitude of 540 miles/ by Rafael
Llerena. [New York], c.1989.
Color; 61.0 x 46.0 cm.
C-P683N74:N4C68/f-1 no. 1

144. Cuba: 28,000 fusilados. Basta ya! Abdala. [Miami, Fla?
1987].
Color; 53 x 40.1 cm.
C87-2-PO-34

145. The Cuban American National Convention. Verbena 89.
Hacienda Mardenpaz... Septiembre 24, 1989. Sponsored by...
[Artist]: Gainza 1989.
Color; 68.7 x 48.3 cm.
[Festival which took place in Hacienda Mardenpaz (owned by
Eduardo Martínez), sponsor of different festivals at his
ranch in South Miami].
C-P683F44:M5F313/f-1 no. 3

146. Cuban artists: Fourth year at the University of Miami.
International Student Lounge, Student Union. Presented by
the Federation of Cuban Students. November 1-5, 1976.
[Coral Gables, Univ. of Miami], 1976.
Color; 43.0 x 24.0 cm.
C-P683F44:C67U55F4E9/f-1 no. 1

147. The Cuban Human Right Film Project presents a film by
      Néstor Almendros, Jorge Ulla. "Nobody Listened." Associate
      producer: Marcelino Miyares, Albert Jolis, Jorge A.
      Rodríguez. Director of photography: Orson Ochoa. Editing:
      Gloria Piñeiro, Esther Durán. Armando Valladares, Eduardo
      Capote [et al]. Reboiro. [New York?], 1987.
      Color; 99.5 x 64.8 cm.
      C-P683F44:M5F513C2/f-1 no. 4

148. Cuban images in Miami. The Grinter Galleries. March 23-
      April 20, 1984. A photo essay by: The Cuban-American
      Student Association, Co-Sponsor: The Center for Latin
      American Studies. [Miami, Fla.], 1984.
      B&w; 45.3 x 35.5 cm.
      C-P683F44:M5L6/f-1 no. 2

149. The Cuban Museum of Art and Culture, June 7-August 2, 1986.
      Mira! The Canadian Club Hispanic Art Tour. New York, Los
      Angeles, San Francisco, Denver, Houston, Miami, Chicago.
      1985, 1986, 1987. [Illustration]: "El Pantalón Rosa" by
      César Martínez. [New York, 1985?]
      Color; 76.0 x 61.0 cm.
      C-P683F44:M5M813M8/f-1 no. 1

150. Cubano, acto masivo, sábado, octubre 21, 2:00 p.m.
      Monumento Maceo, calle 9 y avenida 13 SW, la lucha
      continúa, Abdala... [Miami, FL, 1978.]
      B&w; 43 x 28 cm.
      C87-2-PO-20

151. Cubano - Defiende a los mambises encarcelados en Nueva
      York. Exige justicia para Ramón S. Sánchez y sus
      compañeros. Organización para La Liberación de Cuba (OPLC)
      [New York?: OPLC, n.d.]
      B&w; 44.7 x 28.7 cm.
      C-P683N74:N4C7/f-1 no. 1

152. ¡Cubano! ¡El grito de la guerra nos llama! ¡La hora
      llegó! Estamos en los principios...[Artist]: Caldevilla.
      [Miami, Fla.], 1981.
      Color; 59.6 x 43.0 cm.
      C-P683F44:M5L45C8/f-1 no. 2

153. Cubano! El pueblo convoca al pueblo, Marcha de la
      Integridad Cubana. Sábado, mayo 7, hora 3 p.m. Lugar:
      Monumento Mártires de Girón... al parque José Martí. La
      Independencia no se obtiene dependiendo. [Miami, Fla.:
      Marcha de la Integridad Cubana], 1988.
      Color; 43.2 x 28.0 cm.
      C-P683F44:M5L45C8/f-1 no. 10

154. Cubano exilado: esperamos por ti. Cubano: "Es inmoral no
estar en nada." Crees tu bien, que mientras tus
familiares, amigos o compatriotas se hallan en prisión hay
gente aquí sin hacer nada?... [Miami] : Nacionalismo
Realista, [n.d.]
B&w; 35.2 x 21.9 cm.
C-P683F44:M5L45C8/f-1 no. 1

155. Cubano, por la libertad marcha a Washington, 20 de mayo,
1972. [New Jersey, 1972].
B&w; 28 x 21.5 cm.
C87-2-PO-5

156. Cubano, tu contribución es decisiva. Radio maratón, lunes
30 de enero. Coalición Nacional por una Cuba Libre.
[Miami, Fla.] : Pac, [n.d.]
Color; 56.0 x 35.7 cm.
C-P683F44:M5R313/f-1 no. 2

157. ¡Cubano! Unete a los tuyos. Pertenece a la reserva
militar revolucionaria de la OPLC, Organización para la
Liberación de Cuba... [Miami, Fla.?] : OPLC; [n.d.]
Color; 43.2 x 28.0 cm.
C-P683F44:M5L4C8/f-1 no. 4

158. Cubanos, con tres actos conmemorando "Abdala" el 27 de
noviembre. En Miami, en el Bayfront Park. En Washington,
frente a la Casa Blanca. En New York, frente a las
Naciones Unidas y a la Delegacion Castro-Comunista...
[Designer: Luis Fernández-Puente. New York, ca. 1973].
B&w; 42 x 28 cm.
C87-2-PO-8

159. Cubanos: El tañido de tu "gloriosa campaña" toca de nuevo a
rebato al patriotismo y dignidad. 10 de octubre 1868. La
Demajagua - 10 de octubre 1968. Stadium 10 de octubre.
Convocan: Veteranos de la Independencia de Cuba. [Miami,
Fla.], 1968.
B&w; 43.0 x 27.8 Cm.
C-P683F44:M5A3813D5/f-1 no. 1

160. Cubanos, por la libertad e independencia de Cuba,
conmemoremos el natalicio de José Martí, sábado enero 25, 8
p.m. Koubek Center... que ningún cubano falte, Abdala...
[Miami, Fl, ca. 1977].
Color; 35.5 x 22 cm.
C87-2-PO-15

161. Cubanos, por todos los mártires de nuestras luchas, de ayer
y de hoy, por la libertad e independencia de Cuba.
Conmemoremos el natalicio de José Martí, sábado enero 20, 8

p.m. Iglesia San Agustín, New York Avenue. Esquina a
Calle 40, Union City, NJ, que ningún cubano falte, el
futuro será nuestro, Abdala... [Poster taken as model for
Marti commemoration in other towns. Union City, NJ, 1977].
B&w; 40.5 x 24 cm.
C87-2-PO-16

162. Cuentos de amor... y Cuba. Concierto con la música de
Solange Lasarte. Narrador: Ramón González Cuevas. Sobre
un guión de Ma. Julia Casanova. Cantantes: Chamaco García,
Tania Martí [et al]. Dirección musical: Baserva Soler.
Actuación especial: Manolo Fernández. Auditorium: Koubek
Memorial Center, University of Miami... [Miami, Fla., n.d.]
B&w; 35.7 x 21.3 cm.
C-P683F44:M5C8C613K6/f-1 no. 2

163. Dade County Auditorium. Alberto Morgan y A-1 Productions
Presentan: Ochún Obbayeye. Obra Musical afro-cubana.
Romántica leyenda del folklore cubano. Coreografía y
dirección artistica: Alberto Morgan. Dirección de escena
y diseños: José M. Coro. Asistente de dirección: Yuyo.
Protagonista: Juanita Baró... [Miami, Fla., n.d.]
Sepia; 28.0 x 21.5 cm.
C-P683F44:M5F613/f-1 no. 2

164. Dador ediciones, Rafael Rosado, Esperando la flecha...
Reinaldo Arenas, La Loma del Angel... Carlos Montenegro,
Hombres sin mujer... Próximas apariciones: El espectador y
los signos/ ensayo/ Nilo Palenzuela. Mi tío el empleado/
narrativa/ Ramón Meza. Las voces encontradas/ poesía/ Ana
Nuño. Memoria y esplendor/ poesía/ Jose Triana. Policrom.
[Miami, Fla., n.d.]
Color; 48.0 x 32.8 cm.
C-P683F44:M5M413B6/f-1 no. 9

165. Danilo Bardisa presents "The Worms, Los Gusanos." Teatro
Trail. Estreno mundial. Desde nov. 3. A Camilo Vila Film.
Starring Orestes Matachena, Mario Peña, [et al]. Produced
by: Danilo Bardisa. Directed by Camilo Vila. Screenplay by
Danilo Bardisa and Camilo Vila. Based on a play by Eduardo
Corbe. Cinematography by Ramón Suárez, music score by José
Raúl Bernardo. [Miami, Fla.], South American Shorts,
c.1977.
Color; 71.3 x 55.8 cm.
C-P683F44:M5F513C2/f-1 no. 1

166. La Danza y Ma. Julia Casanova presentan: Corona de amor
desde septiembre 5, 1982. Protagonizada por Aurora
Collazo, Julia Menéndez. En sept., Raul Dávila. Oct. y
nov., Evelio Taillacq, Carlos Poce, Reny González, Ma.
Elena Sánchez Ocejo, José Amaya. Dirección: Ma. Julia

Casanova. [Miami, Fla.], Cortesía de Casa Capó. [1982?].
B&w; 41.5 x 26.7 cm.
C-P683F44:M5T513T44/f-1 no.1

167. "The Day After Valentines". Erotic, nostalgic, romantic,
      art. By: Tony Allegro, Margarita Cano [et al].
      Performance/Opening, February 15, 1985. Robin Lanvin
      Gallery. Poster design: Rick García. [Miami, Fla.], 1985.
      Color; 63.7 x 48.5 cm.
      C-P683F44:M5T513/f-1 no. 9

168. De la literatura considerada como una forma de urticaria,
      Carlos Alberto Montaner. Nova Scholar: Una colección
      monográfica dedicada a escritores españoles e
      hispanoamericanos... [Artist] : Tony Evora. Madrid:
      Editorial Playor, [n.d.].
      Color; 57.5 x 33.9 cm.
      C-P683F44:M5M413B6/f-1 no. 2

169. X Feria de los Municipios de Cuba en el Exilio. Flagler
      Dog Track... Miami, Fl. Abril 9-12, '92. "Unidos en la fe
      y la esperanza." [Sponsors] : El Nuevo Herald, Florida
      Lottery, Budweiser, WLTV 23, Goya, WQBA. [Miami, Fla.],
      1991.
      Color; 39.9 x 60.9 cm.
      C-P683F44:M5F4M7/f-1 no. 9

170. Desfile de la Hispanidad, Quinta Avenida, 11 de octubre
      '81. [Artist] : Pier. [New York?] : SIN Inc., c.1981.
      Color; 80.5 x 65.5 cm.
      C-P683N74:N4F4H5/f-1 no. 1

171. Día Internacional de la Solidaridad Anticomunista. En
      homenaje a los combatientes afganos. Agrupación Abdala.
      Hotel Palace, Salón Andora, Isla Verde, Puerto Rico,
      diciembre 5, 1982, 8 p.m. [Artist] : David Medina,
      Inscribed by author to the University of Miami Library.
      [San Juan, P.R.], 1982.
      Color; 61.0 x 44.0 cm.
      C-P683F44:M5A713M4/f-1 no. 1

172. Día Internacional de Solidaridad con los asilados del Perú.
      Felino Ramírez Batista, Eduardo Herrera Díaz, Pedro
      Betancourt Collazo. Tres de abril de mil novecientos
      ochenta y siete. [Miami, Fla?], 1987.
      Color; 43.1 x 28.0 cm.
      C-P683F44:M5P7713P4/f-1 no. 1

173. Diario Libre con "El Sobre de la sorpresas." Ahora en
      grande. ¡Pídelo aquí! .25. [Miami, Fla., n.d.]
      Color; 54.5 x 39.5 cm.

C-P683F44:M5M413/f-1 no. 4

174. Días de carnaval, noches de Lowenbrau. Festival de la Calle
     Ocho, marzo 9, 1986. Calle 8 y la 7 Ave. Charytín, Willie
     Colón, Carlos Mata, Oscar de Fontana, Las Chicas Canela.
     [Miami, Fla.,] 1986.
     Color; 12.3 x 81.3 cm.
     C-P683F44:M5F4C3/f-2 no. 19

175. Diciembre 9, dia internacional de los derechos humanos.
     Cubano, protesta... [New Jersey, 1976].
     Color; 46 x 31 cm.
     C87-2-PO-14

176. "Las Diego" en concierto, fuga, voz, y movimiento. Dade
     County Auditorium. Locutores: Néstor Cabel y Aleida Leal.
     Artista invitado: Gustavo Rojas. Elenco artístico: Giselle,
     Ricardo Juan, Erlinda de Armas. Con la participación de
     bailarines del "Ballet Etudes Co..." Fotos: Mercy. Fechas:
     15 mayo, 17 mayo. [Miami, Fla., 1981].
     Color; 67.5 x 49.3 cm.
     C-P683F44:M5C8C613/f-2 no. 19

177. 10 de Febrero estreno en este teatro de la película "Los
     Chistes de Alvarez Guedes". Los que tanto han hecho reír en
     discos, ahora en el cine. [Miami, Fla., n.d.]
     Color; 21.5 x 14.0 cm.
     C-P683F44:M5F513/f-1 no. 1

178. A different slice of the apple! Hispanic Arts. Dance...
     Music... Theatre... Visual arts... The poster was made
     possible with public funds from the National Endowment for
     the Arts... Design: Hernández-Porto. New York, [n.d.].
     B&w; 28.0 x 71.2 cm.
     C-P683N74:N4A76/f-1 no. 1

179. Directamente de España, la obra cumbre de Santiago
     Moncada... AMA presenta a la primerísima actriz Amparo
     Rivelles en la audaz comedia, Salvar a los delfines...
     Escenografía y vestuario: Antonio... Dade County
     Auditorium. Única función Agosto 19... [Miami, Fla., n.d.]
     B&w; 35.5 x 21.2 cm.
     C-P683F44:M5T513/f-1 no. 2

180. Distrito 113, Pequeña Habana. Marina. Tu representante
     estatal. Republicano. Pd. Pol. Adv. E.L. Marina Campaign
     Fund. [Miami, Fla., n.d.]
     Color; 57.5 x 37.2 cm.
     C-P683F44:M5P513H68/f-1 no. 5

181. Do you know what is happening inside Cuba? Where the

Communist claws are bleeding thousands of humans to death.
No freedom of speech of press... Are the Cubans going to be
forgotten again? Union City, N.J.: Bloque Cubano de
Organizaciones Revolucionarias. [n.d.]
B&w; 30.5 x 21.5 cm.
C-P683F44:M5A513/f-1 no. 5

182. El Dr. Ismael Hernández & Pasteur Medical Centers presentan
a Evelio Taillacq en su obra "Yo Quiero Ser." Evelio
Taillacq en su gran espectáculo unipersonal. Domingo 21 de
julio, 1991 5:00pm. Teatro Manuel Artime... [Miami, Fla.:
Pasteur Medical Centers], 1991.
Color; 27.9 x 43.2 cm.
C-P683F44:M5T513/f-2 no. 11

183. Dole. Calle Ocho Carnaval. Marzo 1986, Miami, Florida.
Dole Fruit 'n Juice Bars. Dole Fruit and Cream Bars. Design
by Marcelo Rossetti. [S.l.] : Dole Fruit and Cream Bars,
1986.
Color; 54.0 x 42.0 cm.
C-P683F44:M5F4C3/f-2 no. 14

184. Domingo 18 de julio 1932-1982. Bodas de Oro con el teatro
de Pepa Berrio y Rolando Ochoa. Dade County Auditorium...
Gran desfile de estrellas. [Miami, Fla] : International
Medical Centers HMO [1982].
B&w; 55.0 x 38.5 cm.
C-P683F44:M5S413M6/f-1 no. 1

185. Domingo julio 31. Dia de solidaridad con los patriotas
anticommunistas nicaragüenses, [Miami, Fla., n.d.]
Color; 56.0 x 36.0 cm.
C-P683F44:M5F717S6/f-1 no. 1

186. Downtown Summer Festival, August 16, 1981. [Designed by]:
Ditsy. [Miami, Fla.], 1981.
Color; 28.5 x 21.8 cm.
C-P683F44:M5F4D6/f-1 no.3

187. Downtown Summer Festival, August 16, 1981. Hurricane
Dennis [changed to] Sunday August 30. [Miami, Fla.], 1981.
Color; 51.8 x 40.0 cm.
C-P683F44:M5F4D6/f-1 no.5

188. Downtown Summer Festival "Main Street of the Americas,"
August 3, 1980. [Miami, Fla.], 1980.
Color; 30.5 x 23.0 cm.
C-P683F44:M5F4D6/f-1 no. 1

189. During the first annual Hispanic Theatre Festival Prometeo
presents Suicide in Springtime by Alejandro Casona. May 23

and 24 1986. Auditorium, Miami-Dade Community College,
Wolfson Campus. [Miami, Fla.], 1986.
Color; 35.5 x 21.7 cm.
C-P683F44:M5F4H6/f-1 no. 1

190.   ECL/CIELO Comité de Intelectuales y Escritores Libres de
        Oposición. Human Rights Alert. Sebastián Arcos Cazabón,
        27 years old. Ex-political prisoner for attempting to flee
        Cuba... Sebastián is denied... For more information: María
        J. Cazabón, Miami, Fl. [Miami, Fla., n.d.]
        B&w; 35.5 x 21.6 cm.
        C-P683F44:M5P6613C8/f-1 no. 3

191.   8:00 p.m., March 7th, 1986, on Calle Ocho; tension builds
        up... The Miami Herald, Kiwanis, Bud Light, Miami Runners
        Club, Comprehensive American Care, Eastern. A Kiwanis of
        Little Havana event. Design by Rubén Travieso. Art by Pedro
        Astudillo. Miami, Fla., 1986.
        Color; 66.0 x 48.0 cm.
        C-P683F44:M5F4C3/f-2 no. 15

192.   Elect Farina Dade County judge. County wide vote. Pd.
        Pol. Adv. Bob Williamson, Treas., [Miami, Fla. 1990].
        Color; 36.0 x 56.0 cm.
        C-P683F44:M5P513J87/f-1 no. 1

193.   Elect Frank Díaz Silveira, state senator, Dist. 34
        Republican Pd. Pol. Adv. [Miami, Fla., 1982].
        Color, Silkscreen; 56.0 x 35.6 cm.
        C-P683F44:M5P513S48/f-1 no. 1

194.   Elect Lucrecia Granda Dade County court judge. Vote Sept.
        2. Ponche el #223. Pd. Pol. Adv. [Miami, Fla., 1990].
        Color; 43.5 x 28.0 cm.
        C-P683F44:M5P513J87/f-1 no. 2

195.   Elect Manuel Iglesias. Republican, District 18. September
        7, Primary. Congress. Paid for Iglesias Campaign
        Committee. [Miami, Fla., n.d.]
        Color; 44.8 x 34.0 cm.
        C-P683F44:M5P513H68/f-1 no. 3

196.   Elect Rudy Sorondo circuit court judge Sept. 4 Punch #
        149. Pd. Pol. Adv., Pd. for by the Campaign of Rudy
        Sorondo... [Miami, Fla?]: Tim-Cor Poly-Art, [1990].
        Color; 56.0 x 35.4 cm.
        C-P683F43:D3P513J87/f-1 no. 1

197.   En Cuba en la época de Machado hubo in ciclón más fuerte
        que el del '26... Se llamó Filomena. Internacional Art
        Center y El Teatro Bellas Artes presentan a Marta Velasco,

197. En Cuba en la época de Machado hubo un
ciclón más fuerte que el del '26... Se llamó
Filomena. Miami, Fla., n.d.

Emiliano Diez. Todo el Cerro comenta... La vida, pasión, y muerte de Filomena Martínez... Dirección Eduardo Corbe. Teatro de Bellas Artes... Viernes y sábado 9 p.m., domingo 3 p.m. [Miami, Fla., n.d.]
C-P683F44:M5T513T42/f-1 no. 6

198. En el canario amarillo que tiene el ojo tan negro. Cultivo una rosa blanca. Mijares. 1970. [Miami, Fla.] : Mnemosyne Publishing Co., Inc. 1970.
Color; 85.2 x 58.6 cm.
C-P683F44:M5A713M5/f-1 no. 1

199. En el 88 con Budweiser en la Calle Ocho. [Design by] Roblán. Michelob paseo, domingo, 6 marzo, Hansel y Raúl, Carlos Oliva y Los Sobrinos del Juez. Calle Ocho Open House, Celia Cruz con Orquesta Inmensidad, Hansel & Raúl y su Orquesta Calle Ocho, Gilberto Santa Rosa. [Miami, Fla., 1988].
Color; 62.0 x 47.0 cm.
C-P683F44:M5F4C3/f-4 no. 39

200. "En la voz de mi guitarra". Festival celebrando las "Bodas de Oro" (50 años) con el arte del trovador Servando Díaz. Gran desfile artístico. Casa Cuba, 25 de junio 8:00 p.m. [San Juan, P.R.]: Impreso en Express Prints, Inc. [1987?]
Color; 61.0 x 46.8 cm.
C-P633P81:F4A513/f-1 no. 1

201. Enciende, arranca y gana con Newport. Tu puedes ser el feliz ganador de este convertible Dodge Dakota del 1990. Kings Newport, lleno de gusto! Se exhibirá en la Calle 8 Open House junto a la camioneta musical de Newport en la avenida 24... [Miami, Fla.], Lorillard, Inc., 1990.
Color; 45.7 x 45.7 cm.
C-P683F44:M5F4C3/f-7 no. 66

202. Entre rimas y música. Concierto con la poesía de GALA y la música de Solange Lasarte. Actuación estelar de Hada Béjar y Gabriel Casanova, Ileana Cabañas, Tania Martí, Martica Ruíz, Ramón González Cuevas, Antonio Curbelo, Armando Rodríguez. Acompañamiento musical de César Morales, domingo 9 de diciembre. Miami Senior High Auditorium. [Miami, Fla., n.d.]
B&w; 43.0 x 27.9 cm.
C-P683F44:M5C8C613/f-1 no. 5

203. Esa muchacha de ojos café. Ricardo Montaner, Melissa, José Alberto Mugrabi. [Caracas, Venezuela, 1987?]
Color; 59.6 x 44.5 cm.
C-P693V41:T4/f-1 no. 1

204. Escaping from paradise. Cuba. 1980. David Medina.
 [Miami, Fla, 1989?]
 B&w; 60.0 x 45.8 cm.
 C-P683N74:N4M3/f-1 no. 1

205. Escuche el Noticiero Nacional Realista en los 1140 kc. de
 la WMIE a las 6:30 p.m. Nosotros lo haremos. La tesis de
 la indignidad... Y la tesis de la dignidad. Los "líderes"
 de ahora dicen... Antonio Maceo dijo... [Miami, Fla.,
 196-?]
 Sepia; 35.5 x 21.8 cm.
 C-P683F44:M5R313/f-1 no. 4

206. La Escuela de Arte Dramático "Prometeo" del Miami-Dade
 Community College Downtown Campus presenta "El juicio
 final" de José de Jesús Martínez. Sábado, octubre 12, 1974
 en el Miami-Dade Community College, DC Auditorium...
 [Miami, Fla., 1974].
 B&w; 43.0 x 27.7 cm.
 C-P683F44:M5T613P7/f-1 no. 3

207. España de cal y luto. Antonio Durán. Bacardí Art Gallery,
 June 26-July 15, 1978. [Miami, Fla.], 1978.
 B&w; 69.0 x 45.5 cm.
 C-P683F44:M5C8A7B3/f-2 no. 12

208. Los Españolísimos de Raymond y José María presentan:
 Pasodoble, Te quiero. Andrés García Lorca, Galechka,
 Patricia Gallardo. Acompañado por un cuerpo de baile con
 guapísimas chicas. Coreografía: Paco del Puerto. Teatro
 Martí. [Miami, Fla.] : AAA Printing [n.d.]
 B&w; 43.0 x 27.9 cm.
 C-P683F44:M5C8M813/f-1 no. 2

209. Espectacular Década 40 presenta "Aniversario Musical de
 Oro" de Mario Fernández Porta... La madrina de la Década:
 Olga Guillot... Diseño de posters y programas: Manolo
 Espinosa. Producción: Enrique Beltrán. Dirección de
 escena: Mario Martín. Dade County Auditorium, domingo 17
 de mayo de 1987. [Miami, Fla.], 1987.
 B&w; 35.5 x 21.5 cm.
 C-P683F44:M5F4A513/f-1 no. 1

210. Esta si que es... ¡La que se ganó el ño! Cerveza Latina
 Beer. [Miami, Fla., 1987?]
 Color; 64.3 x 49.0 cm.
 C-P683F44:M5M413B4/f-1 no. 3

211. "Estoy orgulloso de representar el corazón de la Pequeña
 Habana." Humberto Cortina. La Pequeña Habana. Vote
 Cortina representante estatal. Distrito 113 - Republicano.

Pagado por la Campaña para Elegir a Cortina.   Tesorero:
Carlos Benítez.   [Miami, Fla., n.d.].
Color; 56.0 x 35.5 cm.
C-P683F44:M5P513H68/f-1 no. 4

212.   An evening with Marta Pérez. Proudly presented by Silva
       Enterprises. Gusmán Philharmonic Hall, Miami, Florida,
       Saturday eve., May 11, 1974. [Miami, Fla.: Silva
       Enterprises], 1974.
       Color: 29.8 x 18.4 cm.
       C-P683F44:M5C8C613/f-1 no. 7

213.   El evento artístico del año, Virginia Alonso en "María
       Grever" con Gustavo Rojas, Elodia Ríovega, Carlos Poce,
       María de los Angeles Montoya, Martica Ruiz y los niños.
       Libreto original y dirección: Mario Martín. Producción:
       Enrique Beltrán. Dirección musical: Jesús García. Dade
       County Auditorium, sábado 29 de noviembre de 1986, domingo
       30 noviembre de 1986. [Miami, Fla.] 1986.
       Color; 30.9 x 21.8 cm.
       C-P683F44:M5C8Z313/f-1 no. 1

214.   Evocación. Concierto a beneficio Sociedad Artístico
       Cultural de las Américas. Sábado, mayo 1, 1976...
       Actuación especial del Coro de Madrigalistas bajo la
       dirección del maestro Manuel Ochoa. Animadora: Geraldine.
       Teatro Lecuona, sábado, mayo 1, 1976. [Miami, Fla.], 1976.
       Sepia; 43.0 x 27.8 cm.
       C-P683F44:M5C8C613/f-2 no. 11

215.   An exciting evening with Rosita Kerr, Cuban pianist, and
       Andrzej Anweiler, Polish-American pianist. Music from
       Poland, Spain, Cuba, United States. Gusman Philharmonic
       Hall, Saturday evening, June 14, 1975. [Artist] : Sonia
       Soberón. [Miami, Fla.], 1975.
       Sepia; 32.5 x 21.5 cm.
       C-P683F44:M5C8C613/f-1 no. 10

216.   An exhibition of contemporary Cuban artists. Outside
       Cuba/Fuera de Cuba.   Cundo Bermúdez, Mario Carreño, Carmen
       Herrera [et al]... A special project of the Office of
       Hispanic Arts, Mason Gross School of the Arts, Ileana
       Fuentes-Pérez, director. Design by J.H. Porto... This
       exhibition has been made possible with funds from: Rutgers,
       the State University of New Jersey... [Rutgers, N.J. : The
       State Univ. of New Jersey, 1987].
       Color; 95.0 x 37.0 cm.
       A traveling exhibit.
       C-P683F44:M5C8A713/f-2 no. 12

217.   Exhibition of Rare Cuban Books, March 23-30, 1979...

University of Miami Library, Brockway Hall. [Miami, Fla.]:
Museo Cubano de Arte y Cultura, Inc., 1979.
B&w; 50.7 x 76.6 cm.
C-P683F44:M5M813M8/f-1 no. 3

218. Exigimos libertad de presos políticos y sindicales,
libertad sindical, de expresión, de entrada y salida del
país, democracia, justicia social, eliminación aparato
represivo de la seguridad del estado, retorno de las tropas
cubanas en el exterior, por la vigencia de los derechos
humanos, por la soberanía e independencia nacional para la
unidad latinoamericana. [Flushing, NY]: Solidaridad de
Trabajadores Cubanos. Comité en el Exterior, [n.d.]
Color; 44.0 x 32.5 cm.
C-P683F44:M5P6613C8/f-1 no. 2

219. Exilio de Matías Montes Huidóboro. Dirección y montaje:
Dumé. Asesor literario: José Corrales. Con Natacha
Amador, Marcos Casanova, Manolo de la Portilla, Celia Do
Muiño, Rubén Rabasa. Premiere: sábado 19 de marzo...
funciones: marzo 20, 24, 25, 26, 27, 31, abril 1, 2, 3,
Museo Cubano de Arte y Cultura. Afiche: Rafael Mirabal.
[Miami, Fla., n.d.]
Color; 44.4 x 31.7 cm.
C-P683F44:M5T513/f-1 no. 6

220. Experimental music concert with pieces for electric guitar,
piano percussion, and poetry by Armando Tranquilino,
Cecilia Rojo, and Julio Estorino. Featuring Imaginary
Concert no. 3. Visual images: Cecilia Rojo. Kinetic
images: Lisette Alvarez. Koubek Center Auditorium, Sunday,
Jan. 11, 1987. [Miami, Fla.], 1987.
B&w; 35.5 x 21.7 cm.
C-P683F44:M5C8C613K6/f-1 no. 1

221. Exposición de dibujo, pintura y escultura. Francisco
Abajo... Miami, Fla.: Asociación Fraternal Latinoamericana,
Inc... 1979.
B&w; 40.5 x 27.7 cm.
C-P683F44:M5C8A713/f-2 no. 11

222. Expresiones Hispanas. The 1988/89 Coors National Hispanic
art exhibit and tour. "Untitled", mixed media. Artist:
José Luis Rodríguez. [Autographed]. Golden, Col.: Adolph
Coors Co., 1989.
Color; 51.0 x 56.0 cm.
C-P683F44:M5F4H5/f-1 no. 10

223. FEC presents Three Days of Cuban Culture. Tues. April 1st-
Thurs. April 3rd. University of Miami Campus. A
spectacular event for no one to miss, by Ali. [Designed by

Ana R. Nuñez. Coral Gables, Fla.: University of Miami, 1980.
B&w; 43.2 x 27.8 cm.
C-P683F44:C67U55F4E9/f-1 no. 2

224. La "Fabim" presenta "Super show del siglo." Payasos, mago, doble programa de baseball y la presentación especial del sensacional cantante "Hugo Henríquez" creador de "Te voy a regalar un continente." Interpretando en concierto más de 25 canciones... Domingo 9 de noviembre, Stadium de Miami. Animación: Aleida Leal. [Miami, Fla., n.d.]
Color; 35.5 x 21.5 cm.
C-P683F44:M5C8C613/f-2 no. 12

225. Federación de Estudiantes Cubanos presents "Expresiones". Monday, October 13... Wednesday, October 15... Friday, October 17... Hispanic musical night. Koubek Memorial Center. [Coral Gables, Fla.: University of Miami, n.d.]
B&w; 43.0 x 28.0 cm.
C-P683F44:C67U55F4E9/f-1 no. 6

226. Federación de Estudiantes Cubanos presents "Raíces": A Hispanic Cultural Festival Oct. 11-17... N.Y. Published by Shorewood Reproductions Inc. [n.d.]
B&w; 72.5 x 57.5 cm.
C-P683F44:C67U55F4E9/f-1 no. 3

227. La Federación de Estudiantes Cubanos, Universidad de Miami presenta nuestro recital: Recordando a Cuba con las composiciones de Carlos Ramos y José Garrido. Marzo 20, Koubek Center. [Coral Gables, Fla.: University of Miami, n.d.]
B&w; 35.5 x 21.5 cm.
C-P683F44:C67U55F4E9/f-1 no. 4

228. Federación de Estudiantes Cubanos, Universidad de Miami presenta Semana de la Cultura Cubana: octubre en Cuba. Domingo 26 de octubre 1975. [Coral Gables, Fla.: University of Miami, 1975?]
B&w; 56.0 x 43.2 cm.
Size varies.
C-P683F44:C67U55F4E9/f-1 no. 5

229. Felicidades. Carnaval Miami, décimo aniversario. Newport lleno de gusto los invita! Paseo, marzo 8. Calle Ocho/Open House, marzo 15. Carnaval Miami Little Havana U.S.A. [Miami, Fla., 1986. Designed by]: Carreño.
Color; 45.8 x 45.8 cm.
C-P683F44:M5F4C3/f-4 no. 37

230. Feria Anual de Allapattah, sábado noviembre 8, 1986 de

FESTIVAL DE LAS ARTES

TERCER ANIVERSARIO DEL MARIEL

DOMINGO 21 de Agosto de 1983 10 A.M. a 8 P.M.

TAMIAMI PARK
112 Ave. S.W. y 24 Calle

Pintura   Artesanía   Música
Dibujo   Cerámica   Teatro
Escultura Literatura Ballet
          Fotografía

Co-Patrocinado por

FACE
Facts About Cuban Exiles

Cortesia del Miami Herald

231. Festival de las Artes, tercer aniversario del Mariel. Designed by Pedro Damián. Miami, Fla., 1983.

10:00 a.m. a 10:00 p.m. Curtis Park... presentada por:
Allapattah Business Development Authority y Allapattah
Community Action... [Miami, Fla.], 1986.
Color; 35.6 x 24.1 cm.
C-P683F44:M5F4A3/f-1 no. 1

231.   Festival de las Artes, tercer aniversario del Mariel,
       domingo 21 de agosto de 1983, Tamiami Park. Pintura,
       artesanía, música, dibujo, cerámica, teatro, escultura,
       literatura, ballet, fotografía. Co-patrocinado por FACE,
       Facts About Cuban Exiles. [Designed by Pedro Damián.
       Miami, Fla.] : The Miami Herald Pub. Co., 1983.
       Color; 56.0 x 42.0 cm.
       C-P683F44:M5F4A513M3/f-1 no. 1

232.   ¡Fidel en Miami! No se pierda la magnífica caracterización
       que hace Armando Roblán en la obra original de Alberto
       González: "No hay mal que dure 100 años ni pueblo que lo
       resista". Con Normita Suárez, Miguel de Grandy II, Sergio
       Doré, Jr., El Tadeo, Laura Hevia, y Lidia Hernández...
       Martí Music Hall. Director: Miguel de Grandy II.
       Productor: Ernesto A. Capote... [Miami, Fla. n.d.]
       B&w; 21.7 x 35.5 cm.
       C-P683F44:M5T513T45/f-1 no. 1

233.   Fiesta Guajira. Centro Mater, April 4-5, 1981. [Miami,
       Fla.: Centro Mater], 1991.
       Color; 43.0 x 28.0 cm.
       C-P683F44:M5F313/f-1 no. 1

234.   5th Annual Grand Prix of Miami for the Camel GT
       Championship. Call your travel agent or Eastern for all
       your travel arrangements. March 1, 1987...Official
       sponsors of the Grand Prix... Mazda: Official Car of the
       Grand Prix. [Miami, Fla.] : 1987.
       Color; 61.0 x 45.7 cm.
       C-P683F44:M5G7/f-1 no. 6

235.   5th Annual Hispanic Arts Festival, April 4th-June 29th
       1980. Promoted by the Association of Hispanic Arts... Made
       possible with public funds from New York State Council on
       the Arts [et al] and private funding from Chemical Bank [et
       al]. New York, [1980].
       Color; 28.0 x 71.2 cm.
       C-P683N74:N4A76/f-1 no. 3

236.   La Finca. Fábula musical de Mario Ernesto Sánchez y Luis
       Felipe Roca. Inspirada en la novela de George Orwell
       "Rebelión en la granja"... Mario Ernesto Sánchez,
       dirección... Alina Interián RAS producción. Celebrando el
       2do aniversario del Teatro Avante. Desde el sábado 5 de

238. G. Cabrera Infante. La Habana para un infante difunto. Photographer: Jesse Fernández. Barcelona, 1979.

marzo de 1983... [Miami, Fla.] : RAS Production, 1983.
Color; 41.5 x 26.8 cm.
C-P683F44:M5T513/f-1 no. 4

237. Forum Pro Congreso de Integración Democrática. Por una
patria libre, de compatriotas libres. II Frente Nacional
Escambray. Cantelli. [Miami, Fla., n.d.]
B&w; 35.5 x 31.5 cm.
C-P683F44:M5A4C6/f-1 no. 1

238. G. Cabrera Infante. La Habana para un infante difunto.
Editorial Seix Barral. Foto: Jesse Fernández. Barcelona:
Seix Barral, 1979.
B&w; 64.3 x 44.0 cm.
C-P683F44:M5M413B6/f-1 no. 3

239. La Gran Enciclopedia Martiana. Esta obra es imprescindible
en su hogar... Más de 3,000 pensamientos y citas de Martí.
Desde la calle Paula hasta Dos Ríos se extiende un sueño:
El de Cuba. Más de 45 escritores... Primera y última
edición limitada. Miami,: Editorial Martiana, Inc., [n.d.]
Color; 62.5 x 95.2 cm.
C-P683F44:M5M413B6/f-1 no. 4

240. Gran Reinado Infantil de Simpatía de *El Condado News*
donde serán coronados rey, reina, príncipes y pajes en cada
una de las dos categorías:... [Miami, Fla., 1986?]
B&w; 43.0 x 28.0 cm.
C-P683F44:M5C6513/f-1 no. 1

241. Gran Romería de Primavera del Centro Asturiano de Miami.
Domingo 17 de mayo de 1987 de 11 a.m. a 7 p.m. Entrada
gratis, Parque de la Policía. Comidas, gigantesca paella...
Gran show artístico... [Miami, Fla.] : Banco Pedroso,

[1987].
B&w;35.4 x 21.5 cm.
C-P683F44:M5F4A503/f-1 no. 1

242. Greater Miami Latin Summer Fiesta. Julio 28-agosto 13...
78. P. Del Valle. [Miami, Fla.], 1978.
Color; 84.0 x 59.6 cm.
C-P683F44:M5F4L3/f-1 no. 1

243. Grupo Cañaveral. [Miami, Fla., n.d.]
Color; 63.0 x 45.5 cm.
C-P683F44:M5C8C613/f-3 no. 23

244. El Grupo Cañaveral. Recital de canciones hispanoamericanas. Lugar: Teatro de Bellas Artes. Fecha:
Domingo, 2 de febrero de 1986... [Miami, Fla.], 1986.

Color; 35.5 x 21.5 cm.
C-P683F44:M5C8C613/f-1 no. 2

245. Grupo Cañaveral. Recital de canciones hispanoamericanas.
Programa "Audiciones" Universidad de Miami. Lugar: Koubek
Memorial Center. Fecha: Viernes, 10 de octubre de 1986.
Hora: 8:00 p.m. [Miami, Fla., 1986].
Color; 35.5 x 31.6 cm.
C-P683F44:M5U55K6P7/f-1 no. 1

246. El grupo teatral "Marcelo Salinas" presenta: "Ven conmigo y
verás La Habana" de José V. Quiroga, la divertida comedia
de la Cuba de ayer... Dirección: Jorge Gómez... Miami High
Auditorium, domingo, marzo 2... [Artist] : R. Delfín
[Miami, Fla.], 1975.
B&w; 43.0 x 28.0 cm.
C-P683F44:M5T613/f-1 no. 3

247. Hacia la guerra por Cuba libre! 1902-1970, 20 de Mayo.
Alcémonos, para la república verdadera... [Miami, Fla.] :
Rex Press, Inc., [1970].
Color; 28.0 x 43.0 cm.
C-P683F44:M5A3813V4/f-1 no. 1

248. Hasta la victoria final venceremos. Cubanos: únanse a la
petición de amnistía general para todos los presos
políticos en cárceles norteamericanas. [Miami, Fla., n.d.]
B&w; 35.5 x 21.5 cm.
C-P681:C7/f-1 no. 2

249. Hernán García. Confidant Birds, oils and inks. Meeting
Point Art Center, September 19, 1981, 6:00 p.m. [Miami,
Fla.], 1981.
Color; 36.0 x 22.5 cm.
C-P683F44:M5C8A713/f-1 no. 6

250. ¡Hijos, ayudénme! ¡La Patria os llama ahora, o nunca!
Para más información comuníquese con los miembros de
Cubanos Unidos. "En Dios confiamos, in God we trust."
[Miami, Fla., n.d.]
Color; 28.0 x 35.5 cm.
C-P683F44:M5L45C8/f-1 no. 6

251. Hispanic Heritage Festival Committee, Inc. A Florida non
profit organization presents: 9 Festival de la Hispanidad,
9th Hispanic Heritage Festival. October 9 to 18, 1981...
Poster designed by: Diane Irene Kachalsky/The Miami
Herald/Creative Services. [Miami, Fla.] : Bellak Color
Corp, 1981.
Color; 88.5 x 57.5 cm.
C-P683F44:M5F4H5/f-1 no. 6

44

255. Hispanic Heritage Festival. Artist: Jorge
Vallina. Miami, Fla., 1987.

252. Hispanic Heritage Festival, Festival de la Hispanidad,
     October 8 to 17, 1982... Poster sponsored by Biscayne
     Bank. Miami 10 Aniversario. Asta. We're glad you're
     coming!... Presented by Hispanic Heritage Festival
     Committee INC. Poster designed by Franco Sierra. [Miami,
     Fla.] Biscayne Bank, 1982.
     Color; 88.5 x 57.5 cm.
     C-P683F44:M5F4H5/f-1 no. 7

253. Hispanic Heritage Festival. Festival de la Hispanidad.
     Miami, Florida. Del 4 al 31 de octubre. October 4 to 31,
     1985. Poster contest sponsored by *The Miami Herald/El
     Nuevo Herald*, Eastern Airlines, & The Equitable Financial
     Services. Artist]: Aldo Amador. 1985. [Miami, Fla.] :
     The Miami Herald Pub. Co., 1985.
     Color; 63.5 x 48.2 cm.
     C-P683F44:M5F4H5/f-2 no. 16

254. Hispanic Heritage Festival, October 1-31, 1986. Official
     poster courtesy of *The Miami Herald/El Miami Herald*.
     [Miami, Fla.] : The Miami Herald Pub. Co., 1986.
     Color; 63.5 x 48.3 cm.
     C-P683F44:M5F4H5/f-1 no. 4

255. Hispanic Heritage Festival, Miami, Florida, del 1 al 31
     de octubre, 1987. 15th Anniversary. Patrocinadores: Board
     and County Commissioners, Council of Arts and Sciences, *The
     Miami Herald/El Nuevo Herald*... Artist: Jorge Vallina.
     [Miami, Fla.] : The Miami Herald Pub. Co., 1987.
     Color; 61.0 x 45.5 cm.
     C-P683F44:M5F4H5/f-1 no. 9

256. Hispanic Heritage Festival. Festival de la Hispanidad.
     Miami, Florida. Del 1 al 31 de octubre/October 1 to 31,
     1988. 1988 official events... [Sponsors]: Board of County
     Commisioners, Metro-Dade, Cultural Affairs Council,
     [et al]. [Miami, Fla.: Hispanic Heritage Council, Inc.],
     1988.
     Color; 44.5 x 53.4 cm.
     C-P683F44:M5F4H5/f-2 no. 14

257. Hispanic Heritage Festival. Festival de la Hispanidad,
     Miami, Florida. Del 1 al 31 de octubre - October 1 to 31,
     1989. Limited collection of the official poster. Courtesy
     of Southeast Bank, *The Miami Herald, El Nuevo Herald*, AT&T
     la mejor decisión. [Miami, Fla.: Hispanic Heritage
     Council, Inc.], 1989.
     Color; 48.8 x 63.5 cm.
     C-P683F44:M5F4H5/f-2 no. 15

258. Hispanic Heritage Festival del 1 al 31 de octubre - October

1 to 31, 1989. Festival de la Hispanidad, Miami,
Florida... Official events... [Miami, Fla.: Hispanic
Heritage Council, Inc.], 1989.
Color; 61.0 x 45.9 cm.
C-P683F44:M5F4H5/f-2 no. 11

259. Hispanic Heritage Festival. Del 1 al 31 de octubre/October
1 to 31, 1990. Limited collection of the official poster
courtesy of Southeast Bank, *The Miami Herald, El Nuevo
Herald*, AT&T la mejor decisión. [Hispanic Heritage
Council, Inc.], 1990.
Color; 48.4 x 63.5 cm.
C-P683F44:M5F4H5/f-2 no. 17

260. Hispanic Heritage Festival Del 1 al 31 de octubre/October 1
to 31, 1991. Hispanic Heritage Council, Inc. 1991.
Sponsors: Board of County Commissioners [et al]. Official
calendar of events... Calendario de eventos... Winning art,
Ricardo González. [Miami, Fla.] : Hispanic Heritage
Council, Inc., 1991.
Color; 45.7 x 61 cm.
C-P683F44:M5F4H5/f-2 no. 20

261. Hispanic Heritage Festival. Festival de la Hispanidad.
Miami, Florida. Del 1 al 31 de octubre/October 1 to 31,
1991. Limited collection of the official poster courtesy
of Southeast Bank, *The Miami Herald, El Nuevo Herald*, AT&T.
[Artist: Ricardo González. Miami, Fla.: Hispanic Heritage
Council, Inc.], 1991.
Color; 45.8 x 61 cm.
C-P683F44:M5F4H5/f-2 no. 18

262. Hispanic Heritage Month, a celebration of Hispanic culture
and history. Miami-Dade Community College recognizes the
contributions of Hispanic heritage with a month long
celebration of all four campuses in honor of Hispanic
culture and history. This calendar was created for your
enjoyment and convenience, so that you may choose from the
diverse events offered by the college during October...
Design by Pierre Pierson. [Miami, Fla.] : MDCC, [n.d.]
Color; 73.2 x 32.3 cm.
C-P683F44:M5F4H5/f-1 no. 1

263. Hispanic Heritage Week. Semana de la Hispanidad, October 7
to 16, 1977... Compliments of the Bank of Miami, Popular
Bank of Miami. [Miami, Fla.] : Office of County
Manager/Communications, 1977.
Color; 84.5 x 54.8 cm.
C-P683F44:M5F4H5/f-1 no. 5

264. Historia gráfica de la auténtica Vírgen de La "Caridad del

266. Honremos a la Virgen de la Caridad. Miami, Fla. n.d.

Cobre." Por la fe y el amor a la Caridad del Cobre.
[Miami, Fla., 197-?]
Color; 22.6 x 36.5 cm.
C-P683F44:M5R4P41308/f-1 no. 6

265. Holiday Merchandise Fair con el Canal 51 y WQBA-AM (La
Cubanísima) presentan a Hilda Carrero, Eduardo Serrano,
Miriam Ochoa. Protagonistas de la novela "Las Amazonas"
Miércoles-jueves-viernes, diciembre 11-12-13, en el Holiday
Merchandise Fair, una de las mayores exhibiciones de
mercancía de alta calidad en E.U. de miércoles a domingo.
Diciembre 11 al 15 en el Centro de Exhibiciones de Coconut
Grove. [Miami, Fla., n.d.]
Color; 43.5 x 28.0 cm.
C-P683F44:M5M413/f-1 no. 1

266. Honremos a la Vírgen de la Caridad asistiendo viernes 8 de
septiembre. Marine Stadium, Key Biscayne... [Miami,
Fla.] : Printed by Dolphin, [n.d.].
Color; 38.7 x 27.9 cm.
C-P683F44:M5M413/f-1 no. 1

267. The Horowitz Collection: rubbings from English Mediaeval
brasses at the Bacardí Art Gallery, 4 march through 31
March, 1983. The Bacardí Art Gallery is a gallery not-for-
profit supported as a community service by Bacardí Imports,
Inc. [Miami, Fla.] : Bacardí Imports, Inc., 1983.
B&w; 43.5 x 41.0 cm.
C-P683F44:M5C8A7B3/f-2 no. 11

268. Humberto Calzada. Forma. 305 Alcazar, Coral Gables. April
10 to May 4, 1981. Autographed Calzada. [Coral Gables,
Fla.], 1981.
Color; 100.5 x 66.0
C-P683F44:M5A713C3/f-1 no. 1

269. INTAR. Hispanic American Theatre (International Arts
Relations Inc.) Max Ferra / Dennis Ferguson-Acosta,
producers. Exiles, a mixed-media musical. [Designed by]
Alberto Barrera. Written by Ana María Simó. Music by
Elliot Sokolov & Louis Milgrom. Directed by María Irene
Fornés. Set by Carlos Almada & Paulette Crowther...
December 9th, through January 2nd, 1983, Intar Stage Two.
[New York, International Arts Relations, Inc.], 1983.
Color; 56.2 x 37.3 cm.
C-P683F44:M5C8M813/f-1 no. 8

270. INTAR. Lydia Cabrera: An Intimate Portrait. Title: Lydia
Cabrera: An Intimate Portrait. Author: Ana María Simó...
Place and date of publication: New York City, May 14,
1984. Publisher: Intar Latin American Gallery. Price:

274.   Improper Conduct.   New York?   1984.

$5.00 plus $1.00 postage and handling. Please send your
orders... [New York: International Arts Relations, Inc.,
1984].
B&w; 27.9 x 21.5 cm.
C-P683F44:M5F613C3/f-1 no. 3

271.   If you think the outlawing of Solidarity and the oppression
       of the Polish people is wrong... Show your support by
       protesting. Solidarnosc. November 10, 1982 at 6 P.M.
       Intersection of S.W. 27th Avenue and 8th Street. Abdala.
       In support of "National Day of Struggle" in Poland.
       [Miami, Fla.], 1982.
       B&w; 42.5 x 27.6 cm.
       C87-2-PO-31

272.   Iliana Krupnik y el Koubek Memorial Center de la
       Universidad de Miami dentro el programa Koubek Cultura 84
       presentan: Hablemos a calzón quitado con Aurelio Paredes,
       Oscar Poveda, Roberto McKay, de Guillermo Gentile.
       Dirigida por: Roberto McKay. Enero 27, 28, 29, 1984.
       Hora, 8:00 p.m. Air Panama International, transportista
       oficial de la compañía. Panamá : Impresora de la
       Nación/INAC, 1983.
       Color; 56.0 x 43.0 cm.
       C-P683F44:M5U55K6C8/f-1 no. 2

273.   Images of Little Havana. Mario Algaze, "Little Havana"/The
       Gallery at General Federal Savings, May 2, 1986. [Miami,
       Fla.], 1986.
       Color; 27.9 x 43.3 cm.
       C-P683F44:M5L6/f-1 no. 1

274.   Improper Conduct, a film by Néstor Almendros and Orlando
       Jiménez Leal. A Cinevista release. "Grand Prix" 12th
       International Human Rights Festival, Strasbourg, 1984.
       [New York?], 1984.
       Color; 89.0 x 58.5 cm.
       C-P683F44:M5F513C2/f-1 no. 3

275.   Los Inocentes. Auditorium del Ada Merritt Community
       School... Libreto: Griselda Noguera, Vivian García.
       Música: Vivian García. Elenco: Minín Bujones, Ana
       Margarita Martínez Casado, Gabriel Casanova, Luis
       Oquendo... Textos citados en libreto y música: Martí,
       Mendive, Palma. Auspiciado por la Sección de Asuntos
       Culturales de la Ciudad de Miami y la cooperación de la
       Escuela Comunitaria Ada Merritt. [Miami, Fla., n.d.]
       B&w; 35.5 x 21.5 cm.
       C-P683F44:M5T613/f-1 no. 1

276.   El Inter Americano Eastern Las Alas de América. Official

Airline of Carnival Miami. Designed by Ruben Travieso, art
by Ruben Travieso and Pedro Astudillo. [Miami, Fla.:
Eastern Airlines, n.d.]
Color; 45.8 x 61 cm.
C-P683F44:M5F4C3/f-8 no. 73.

277. International salsa festival Allapattah USA... (Curtis
park). Fun for the whole family. Dec. 11, 12, 13.
[Miami, Fla., n.d.]
Color; 56.0 x 35.5 cm.
C-P683F44:M5F4M813/f-1 no. 4

278. An invitation to S.W. 8th St. March 14, 1982. Kiwanis of
Little Havana. Calle Ocho Open House, a part of Carnaval
Miami, Little Havana, U.S.A. Souvenir poster courtesy of
The Miami Herald/El Miami Herald. Poster designed by Marta
& Jaime Canavés. [Miami, Fla.] : The Miami Herald Pub.
Co., 1982.
Color; 63.0 x 42.0 cm.
C-P683F44:M5F4C3/f-1 no. 10

279. La Isla. Mar. Washington, D.C. : The Cuban-American
National Foundation, Inc., [n.d.]
Color; 51.0 x 35.5 cm.
C-P683F44:M5C68/f-1 no. 1

280. Iván Acosta en concierto. Canciones de la vida, de la
patria, del amor. Domingo 8 de octubre, 1978, 6:00 p.m.
Presentado por Centro Cultural Cubano de Nueva York.
Auditorium del Planetarium, Museo de Ciencias... [New
York], 1978.
Color; 32.1 x 31.7 cm.
C-P683F44:M5C8C613/f-3 no. 25

281. Jayfran presenta a Dumé interpretando a Eugenio Florit [et.
al.] James L. Knight Center (Ashe Auditorium)...
Septiembre 21, 1991. [Miami, Fla.], 1991.
B&W; 28 x 43.2 cm.
C-P683F44:M5T513/f-2 no. 12

282. Joe Cuba y su sexteto. Nomination Dance May 31 at Hialeah
Auditorium, for president by the salsa party. Let's put a
salsoso in the "White House". Joe Cuba y su sexteto
directamente desde New York con Conjunto Impacto y Conjunto
Universal. Joe Cuba se presentará los días 30 de mayo, 31
de mayo y junio 1 en el Centro Español. [Miami, Fla., n.d.]
B&W; 43.2 x 27.9 cm.
C-P683F44:M5C8M813/f-1 no. 6

283. John J. Koubek Memorial Center. School of Continuing
Studies. J.L. Riera. Miami, June, 1984. [Miami, Fla.],

1984.
Color; 50.7 x 40.5 cm.
C-P683F44:M5C8A713K6/f-1 no. 2

284. John J. Koubek Memorial Center. University of Miami School
of Continuing Studies. Riera. Paintings and sculpture, June
6-June 30, 1984. [Miami, Fla.], 1984.
Color; 64.5 x 43.8 cm.
C-P683F44:M5C8A713K6/f-1 no. 1

285. José Martí [Computer design. Miami, Fla., 1980?]
Color; 60 x 45 cm.
C87-2-PO-26

286. José Martí y los símbolos cubanos. Original: Julio
Guerra/82. [Miami, Fla.], 1982.
Color; 43.2 x 32.0 cm.
C-P683F44:M5M46H613/f-1 no. 2

287. Juana de Arco. Aurora Collazo, Pedro de Pool, Sergio Doré,
Manuel Estanillo [et al]. Actor invitado: Jorge Guerrero.
Actuación especial: Germán Barrios. Versión y dirección:
Yoly Arocha. En el Teatro de Bellas Artes... [Miami, Fla.,
n.d.]
Color; 33.9 x 16.6 cm.
C-P683F44:M5T513T42/f-1 no. 4

288. Julio Larraz at the Bacardí Art Gallery, December 10, 1982
through January 24, 1983. The Bacardí Art Gallery is a
gallery not-for-profit supported as a community service by
Bacardí Imports. "Minaret," oil on canvas, 84 x 66".
[Miami, Fla.: Bacardí Imports, Inc.], 1982.
Color; 51.5 x 30.5 cm.
C-P683F44:M5C8A7B3/f-2 no. 15

289. Kathie y el hipopótamo. Performed in Spanish. Gala
Saturday, November 9, 1985. Guest of honor: The
playwright Mario Vargas Llosa. Reception following.
Director: Istvan Hidvegi... SIBI Cultural Center... Co-
sponsored by the Miami Book Fair International. Lía
Gralletti. [Miami, Fla.], 1985.
Color; 42.5 x 30.5 cm.
C-P683F44:M5T513S5/f-1 no. 1

290. Kiwanis of Little Havana. Calle Ocho, an invitation to S.W.
8th Street Open House, March 6, 1983. Poster compliments of
The Miami Herald. Rubén Travieso '83. [Miami, Fla.] :
Process Color Corporation, 1983.
Color; 46.0 x 58.5 cm.
C-P683F44:M5F4C3/f-2 no. 12

291. Koubek Memorial Center. Escuela de Estudios Continuados.
Universidad de Miami. Como parte del programa Koubek
Cultural Center '83 presenta: Simposium a Salinas, el
sábado 2 de abril de 1983, a las 3:00 p.m. Oradores: Rev.
Marco A. Ramos, Celedonio González, Pedro Leyva, Enrique
Labrador Ruiz, Agustín Tamargo y a Griselda Noguera que
leerá un capítulo de la novela inédita de Marcelo Salinas,
La Olla en la brasa. Homenaje póstumo al poeta, novelista,
ensayista y dramaturgo. [Miami, Fla. : Diseño y
producción: Graphomanía, Inc, 1966].
B&w; 43.0 x 27.7 cm.
C-P683F44:M5U55K6C8/f-1 no. 1

292. Koubek Memorial Center presents Hispanic-American Lyric
Theatre. Great scenes from El Huesped del sevillano, Los
Gavilanes, Naughty Marietta, Marina. Guest artist: Orlando
Hernández. Featuring: Sarah Halley, Jorge Mattox, Carol
González, Ismael González, Robert Heath. Friday, May 29, 8
P.M. Koubek Center Auditorium... Presented with support of
Council of Arts and Sciences, Board of County
Commissioners, Hispanic Heritage Council. [Miami, Fla.:
Hispanic Heritage Council, Inc., n.d.]
Color; 37.1 x 28.0 cm.
C-P683F44:M5T613U5K6/f-1 no. 2

293. Latin U.S.A. Los Angeles, San Antonio, New York, Miami. A
Tale of four cities: Four half hour radio documentaries in
stereo. Produced by Elizabeth Pérez Luna... Through a
grant from the Satellite Program Development Fund /NPR/CPB.
[Philadelphia, 198-?]
Color; 66.0 x 45.7 cm.
C-P683P44:P3R313/f-1 no. 1

294. El León dormido. Gusman Hall, abril 13, 1974. Entrada por
invitación. Miami Dade Community College, Downtown
Campus... Pepa Berrio, Mario Ernesto Sánchez [et al].
[Miami, Fla.], 1974.
Sepia; 60.0 x 42.7 cm.
C-P683F44:M5T513/f-1 no. 8

295. Lever Brothers creadores de Wisk Power Scoop y Snuggle
presentan a Willy Chirino en concierto. En beneficio de
las becas José Martí. Dade County Auditorium. Sábado, 10
de agosto 1991, 8pm... 23 WLTV Miami, Radio Mambí WAQI 710
AM, Radio Ritmo 95.7 FM, Sedano's Supermarkets, DCA Dade
County Auditorium... Photo: Michael Wray. [Miami, Fla.] :
Drago Artistic designs, Inc., 1991.
Color; 91.5 x 59.7 cm.
C-P683F44:M5C8C613/f-4 no. 31

296. La libertad de los mares. Único camino para libertar a

Cuba. Al combate corred bayameses... Brigada de Asalto
2506. [Miami, Fla., n.d.]
Color; 43.0 x 56.0 cm.
C-P683F44:M5L45C8/f-1 no. 7

297. Lincoln Díaz-Balart. Republican state representative.
District 110. Pd Pol Ad. [Miami, Fla., n.d.]
Color; 33.7 x 23.5 cm.
C-P683F44:M5P513H68/f-1 no. 1

298. Lissette en concierto. Viernes, sept. 13, 8:30 p.m.
sábado, sept. 14, 8:30 p.m.... Dade County Auditorium...
[Miami, Fla.] : Discos CBS Internacional, [n.d.]
Color; 44.7 x 33.4 cm.
C-P683F44:M5C8C613/f-3 no. 21

299. Lite Beer te invita a celebrar Calle Ocho. Cerveza
Lite/Super Q Stage con el Gran Combo de Puerto Rico,
Wilfrido Vargas, Roberto Torres y otros. Ven y baila en la
esquina de la Calle Ocho y la Avenida 19. Milwaukee,
Wisconsin : Miller Brewing Company [n.d.].
Color; 76.0 x 50.9 cm.
C-P683F44:M5F4C3/f-5 no. 41

300. Little Havana activities and nutrition centers of Dade
County Inc. y Coors presentan Fiesta 20 de Mayo, May Fest.
Sábado 16... domingo 17... [Miami, Fla., n.d.]
Color; 61.0 x 46.0 cm.
C-P683F44:M5A3813/f-1 no. 2

301. Lowenbrau Grand Prix of Miami. February 22-23, 1986.
Qualifying for the Lowenbrau Grand Prix of Miami Camel GT
pole position. Plus two full days of supporting races.
March 1-2, 1986. Saturday, March 1... Sunday, March 2...
[Miami, Fla.], 1986.
Color; 82.0 x 51.0 cm.
C-P683F44:M5G7/f-1 no. 5

302. Lowenbrau Grand Prix of Miami. Saturday, Feb. 23. "Rose
Auto Qualifying Day"... Sunday, Feb. 24... Watch for the
exciting Mazda Inter American Challenge race on Saturday.
[Artist:] John Rush. [Miami, Fla.: The Miller Brewing Co.,
1987].
Color; 87.0 x 50.9 cm.
C-P683F44:M5G7/f-1 no. 4

303. Lowenbrau saluda a Calle Ocho en su décimo aniversario, 15
de marzo, 1987, Carnaval Miami, Calle Ocho, Miami, Florida.
[Designed by] Otero. [Miami, Fla.], 1987.
Color; 76.0 x 49.5 cm.
C-P683F44:M5F4C3/f-4 no. 35

304. La lucha continúa, Abdala, 9o. Congreso Internacional
     Abdala, julio 27-29, 1979. [Artist, Luis Fernández-
     Puentes]. Miami, Fla., 1979.
     Color; 65 x 48 cm.
     C87-2-PO-23

305. Luis Crespo, un año de martirio, preso y mutilado por
     luchar por Cuba, apoyarlo es deber, Agrupación Abdala.
     [New Jersey, 1974].
     B&w; 43 x 28 cm.
     C87-2-PO-10

306. Lydia Cabrera. Piedras mágicas... Exposición Cuban Women's
     Club, Miami, Florida, abril 15-16-17, 1977. [Miami,
     Fla.], 1977.
     Color; 50.3 x 32.6 cm.
     C-P683F44:M5F613C3/f-1 no. 1-3

307. MIA (oleo). Artista: Adelfa Cantelli. 1971. [Miami, Fla.]:
     The Trust Bank. 1986.
     Color; 27.7 x 33.4 cm.
     C-P683F44:M5A713C35/f-1 no. 1

308. Manicato M Films Inc. presenta un film de Iván Acosta con
     Rubén Rabasa, Reynaldo Medina, [et al]. Escenografía: Siro
     Castillo. Música: Sergio García-Marruz. Edición: Gloria
     Piñeyro. Director de fotografía: Henry Vargas. Productor:
     Camilo Vila. Productor ejecutivo: Marcelino Miyares.
     Escrita y dirigida: Iván Acosta. "Amigos". Desde Oct. 25.
     Teatro Trail. [Miami, Fla.: Manicato M Films, Inc., n.d.]
     Color; 28.3 x 26.8 cm.
     C-P683F44:M5F513/f-1 no. 2

309. Mapa guía Calle 8, 1985. Arte y producción: Rubén
     Travieso, March, 1985. Colaboración y caricaturas:
     Gervasio Esturo. Separación de colores por Process Color.
     Map: c. Marketing Art Promotions & Rubén Travieso.
     Hialeah, Fla.: Central Press, 1985.
     Color; 93.0 x 59.9 cm.
     C-P683F44:M5F4C3/f-3 no. 30

310. Mara y Orlando en concierto "Bajo el cielo de Cuba". Una
     tarde inolvidable con la música, los paisajes, los rincones
     más bellos de la Isla... ¡Una tarde en Cuba! Dirección
     musical: Baserva Soler. Domingo 13 de octubre, Planetarium
     de Miami. [Miami, Fla., n.d.]
     B&w; 35.5 x 23.0 cm.
     C-P683F44:M5C8C613/f-2 no. 14

311. Mara & Orlando en concierto. El miércoles 14 de marzo de
     1984. TBA Teatro de Bellas Artes. [Miami, Fla.], 1984.

B&w; 35.5 x 21.5 cm.
C-P683F44:M5C8C613/f-2 no. 15

312.   Mara y Orlando en concierto. La música cubana olvidada.
       TBA, Teatro de Bellas Artes, domingo 28 de octubre, domingo
       4 de noviembre. [Miami, FL] : AAA Printing, [n.d.]
       B&w; 35.5 x 21.5 cm.
       C-P683F44:M5C8C613/f-1 no. 9

313.   Mara y Orlando. Una tarde con la música de siempre. TBA
       Teatro de Bellas Artes, domingo 21 de abril, domingo 28 de
       abril. [Miami, Fla., n.d.]
       B&w; 35.5 x 21.6 cm.
       C-P683F44:M5C8C613/f-1 no. 8

314.   March 15, 1987. 10th Anniversary. Kiwanis of Little
       Havana. Calle Ocho Open House. Art by Rubén Travieso...
       [Miami, Fla.] : The Miami Herald, 1987.
       Color; 61.5 x 46.0 cm.
       C-P683F44:M5F4C3/f-4 no. 34

315.   March 4, 1984. Celebrate Calle Ocho Open House. Kiwanis of
       LIttle Havana. Poster by Rubén Travieso. [Miami, Fla.] :
       The Miami Herald, 1984.
       Color; 56.7 x 45.0 cm.
       C-P683F44:M5F4C3/f-3 no. 22

316.   The march toward America. "First we will take Eastern
       Europe, then the masses of Asia, then we will slowly
       encircle the last bastion of capitalism (America) and it
       shall fall like an over-ripe fruit," Vladimir Lenin,
       1917... The march continues: Afghanistan... Ethiopia... [et
       al]. "In October 1917 we parted with the Old World,
       rejecting it once and for all. We are moving toward a new
       world, the world of Communism. We shall never turn off
       that road," Mikhail Gorbachev, November 2, 1987...
       [Miami, Fla.] : Conservative Victory Committee, 1987.
       Color; 39.2 x 22.5 cm.
       C-P683F44:M5A513/f-1 no. 7

317.   La marcha de un pueblo en rebeldía. Primer aniversario de
       la Protesta de la Habana. Afirme nuestra determinación a
       ser libres como se demostró en la Embajada del Perú. Desde
       Miami High School... hasta el busto de Maceo. Sábado, 4 de
       abril 1981, 2:00 p.m. [Miami, Fla.] : Agrupación Abdala,
       [1981].
       Color; 57.4 x 37.3 cm.
       C87-2-PO-28

318.   Marzo, mes por la libertad de Orlando Bosch. El exilio lo
       reclama. ALOBO. [Miami, Fla.] : Alianza Libertad Orlando

Bosch, [n.d.]
Color; 44.5 x 29.3 cm.
C-P683F44:M5C7/f-1 no. 1

319.   Las Máscaras presenta: La inolvidable obra de Robert
       Anderson "Te y Simpatía" con Hada Béjar, Alfonso Cremata,
       Salvador Ugarte [et al].   Dirección de Salvador Ugarte.
       Dade County Auditorium, sábado 2 de septiembre...   [Miami,
       Fla.: Patronato del Teatro Las Máscaras, n.d.]
       B&w; 43.0 x 28.3 cm.
       C-P683F44:M5T513M3/f-1 no. 1

320.   Las Máscaras presenta la maravillosa obra de Alejandro
       Casona ¡Aclamada en toda América y Europa! La Dama del
       Alba. Hada Béjar, Aleida Leal, Mary Munné, Salvador
       Ugarte, Alfonso Cremata [et al]. Ada Merritt High School
       Auditorium, sábado 11 de diciembre... [Miami, Fla.:
       Patronato del Teatro Las Máscaras, n.d.]
       Color; 40.7 x 38.6 cm.
       C-P683F44:M5T513M3/f-1 no. 4

321.   Mercadal. April 25, 1981, Gusman Concert Hall, University
       of Miami. "The guitarist Mercadal..." Lecuona Academy of
       the Arts presents Juan Mercadal (guitarist) in a recital of
       guitar favorites. [Miami, Fla.} : Lecuona Academy of the
       Arts, 1981.
       Silkscreen, Color; 42.0 x 26.5 cm.
       C-P683F44:M5C8C613/f-1 no. 1

322.   Las metas, instrumento de trabajo esclavo en Cuba
       comunista... [Miami, Fla., n.d.]
       Color; 73.5 x 49.5 cm.
       C-P683F44:M5C68L3/f-1 no. 1

323.   Mézclate en la Calle Ocho con Smirnoff. Carnival Miami,
       Little Havana U.S.A. Smirnoff Vodka... Ste. Pierre
       Smirnoff Fls. (Division of Heublein, Inc.) Hartford,
       Conn., Heublein, Inc. [1990].
       Color; 56.1 x 43.2 cm.
       C-P683F44:M5F4C3/f-6 no. 60

324.   Miami-Dade Community College, Wolfson Campus. Paella '86,
       the battle of paellas, October 11, 1986. [Miami, Fla.] :
       LDC Graphics, 1986.
       Color; 78.2 x 45.0 cm.
       C-P683F44:M5F4H5P3/f-1 no. 1

325.   Miami-Dade Community College Wolfson Campus Prometeo
       presenta Los Invasores de Egon Wolff. Tercer Festival de
       Teatro, mayo 24-25, 8:30 p.m. Minorca playhouse, Coral
       Gables. [Miami, Fla., 1988].

Color; 35.5 x 21.5 cm.
C-P683F44:M5F4H6/f-1 no. 5

326. Miami Florida U.S.A. 8th Annual Hispanic Heritage Week.
Poster sponsored by Burger King. Metropolitan Dade County
and the Board of County Commissioners, Dade County Council
of Arts and Sciences and the Tourist Development Council
present Hispanic Heritage Week/Semana de la Hispanidad,
October 3-12, 1980. [Designed by]: Eddy Jay. Miami, Fla.:
Office of County Manager /Communications, 1980.
Color; 84.5 x 54.5 cm.
C-P683F44:M5F4H5/f-1 no. 8

327. The Miami Generation, 9 Cuban-American artists, June 11-
August 31, 1984, at Meridian House International. Sponsored
by WLTV Channel 23, Miami and Spanish International
Communications Corporation. Girt with Turbin of a Mondrian,
Emilio Falero. [Miami, Fla., n.d.]
Color; 55.9 x 43.2 cm.
C-P683F44:M5C8A713/f-1 no. 9

328. Miami Grand Prix Club, presented by Perry Ellis. Tan,
don't burn. Original serigraph by Randy Owens [Miami,
Fla.], c.1990.
Color; 56.0 x 49.6 cm.
C-P683F44:M5G7/f-1 no. 9

329. Miami Hispanic Club, Inc. presenta a Miramont Productions
en Ninette y un señor de Murcia. Comedia romántica de
Miguel Mihura, premio "Calderón de la Barca" 1964...
Sábado, sept. 24, 8:30 p.m. Domingo, sept. 25, 3:30 y 8:30
p.m. Goodlet Theatre... [Miami, Fla.] : Miami Hispanic
Club, Inc., [n.d.]
Color; 35.5 x 21.5 cm.
C-P683F44:M5T513/f-1 no. 10

330. Miami is for us. Sidewalk Sam. Limited edition. Carnaval
Miami 1985. [Miami, Fla.], 1985.
Color; 71.0 x 56.0 cm.
C-P683F44:M5F4C3/f-3 no. 29

331. Miami Lyric Group Inc. presents: performed in concert with
piano Lucia Di Lammermoor. Sunday, October 22, 1989 at the
Historic Miami Senior High School Theatre... time 3:00 p.m.
Steven Crawford conducting from the piano, Assistant
conductor of the Greater Miami Opera Association... [Miami,
Fla.] : Miami Lyric Group, Inc., 1989.
C-P683F44:M5C8C613/f-3 no. 27

332. Miami '92. 1492 Encounter of two worlds 1992.
Commemorative poster courtesy of The Miami Herald/El Nuevo
Herald. [Artist]: Carlos Benítez. [Miami] : The Miami
Herald Pub. Co., [1991].

Color; 46 x 61 cm.
C-P683F44:M5F4H5/f-2 no. 19

333. Michelob paseo, domingo, marzo 8. Hansel & Raúl, Roberto
Torres con Alex León y su orquesta. Bud Light 8K Run,
viernes, marzo 13. Bike Dash sábado, marzo 14. Calle Ocho
Open House, Celia Cruz con Orquesta Inmensidad, Hansel y
Raúl y su Orquesta Calle Ocho. Alberto Santa Rosa y su
orquesta. [Art work]: Mike, Sahara, Haydee Scull. [Miami,
Fl] : Drago Artistic Designers, Inc., [n.d.]
Color; 62.5 x 47.0 cm.
C-P683F44:M5F4C3/f-4 no. 36

334. 1868-1967. 10 de octubre. Carlos M. de Céspedes, Padre de
la Patria. ¡Sacrificó su hacienda...! ¡Ofrendó su vida en
holocausto a la libertad...! La grandeza de su alma fue su
patriotismo, desinterés y amor a Cuba! Printing paid by
Miami Quality Shoes. [Miami] : Rex Press Inc. [1967].
Color; 33.0 x 21.5 cm.
C-P683F44:M5A3813D5/f-1 no. 2

335. Miller High Life Beer. A gozar con la cerveza Miller! En la
Calle Ocho el 14 de marzo. Con las orquestas Miami Sound
Machine y Salsa Express. Música, diversión, regalos. If
you've got the time, we've got the beer. Milwaukee,
Wisconsin : Miller Brewing Company, 1981.
Color; 35.5 x 27.8 cm.
C-P683F44:M5F4C3/f-1 no. 8

336. Miller High Life Beer. Bienvenidos, marzo 8 en la Calle 8.
Miami Sound Machine y Salsa Express. Música, diversión,
regalos. If you've got the time, we've got the beer.
Milwaukee, Wisconsin: Miller Brewing Company, 1981.
Color; 40.5 x 28.0 cm.
C-P683F44:M5F4C3/f-1 no. 7

337. Miller High Life y Super Q presentan Cheo Feliciano con la
Típica Tropical y la Tremenda, en la Calle Ocho, el domingo
6 de marzo. Música, alegría, regalos y un incomparable
show aéreo con El Escuadrón Aéreo Miller. [Milwaukee,
Wis.: Miller Brewing, Co., n.d.]
Color; 56.5 x 44.0 cm.
C-P683F44:M5F4C3/f-1 no. 3

338. Miller High Life y Super Q presentan Ray Barreto y Charanga
América, en la Calle Ocho. 17 Avenida y la Calle 8, la
estación de gasolina Gulf, el domingo 6 de marzo. Música,
alegría y regalos. Ven, es la hora Miller. [Milwaukee,
Wis.: Miller Brewing Co., n.d.]
Color; 56.5 x 43.5 cm.
C-P683F44:M5F4C3/f-1 no. 2

339. El mito, la música, el dolor, la mujer, la verdad, Sonia Barrel en Piaf, la historia verdadera de Pam Gems (Premio Tony 1981). Versión y dirección: Gonzalo Rodríguez. Febrero 1985, Teatro de Bellas artes. [Miami, Fla.], 1985.
B&w; 34.7 x 21.3 cm.
C-P683F44:M5T513T42/f-1 no. 1

340. "The Moorish Eye", oils on clay by Paquita Parodi. May 7 through June 10, 1982, Forma Gallery. Champagne opening, May 7, 7-10 p.m. 305 Alcazar. Coral Gables, Fla., [n.d.]
Color; 61.0 x 45.8 cm.
C-P683F44:M5C8A713/f-1 no. 8

341. Motivación e inspiración del paisaje. El crepúsculo extiende su manto... Orlando Bosch. Prisión San Carlos de Caracas. O. Bosch. [Miami, Fla.?], 1981.
Color; 45.7 x 60.5 cm.
C-P683F44:M5A713B6/f-1 no. 3

342. Movimiento de Solidaridad Militante con los Municipios de Cuba en el Exilio, dirección de orientación gestora. Municipios-Exilio, en esta casa hay sitio para usted. " El municipio es la raiz y la sal de la libertad," José Martí... Transmitiendo para Cuba y el exilio todos los días FNCA, Radio Martí, Unión Radio... Cuando estarán todos juntos? 1959-1988. [Miami, Fla.], 1988.
Color; 21.5 x 35.6 cm.
C-P683F44:M5L45C8/f-1 no. 9

343. Municipios de Cuba en el Exilio. Abril 6-10. Relación de los municipios cubanos... Segunda Feria Nacional. Arte, música, tradiciones. Second National Fair of the Cuban Municipalities. Art, music, traditions. April 6-10... [Miami, Fla.] : The Miami Herald Pub. Co., [1983].
Color; 45.5 x 61.0 cm.
C-P683F44:M5F4M7/f-1 no. 3

344. Municipios de Cuba en el Exilio. Orange Bowl, abril 5-8. Relación de municipios cubanos... Segunda Feria Nacional. Arte, música, tradiciones. Second National Fair of the Cuban Municipalities. Art, music, traditions. April 5-8. [Miami, Fla.] : The Miami Herald, [1983].
Color; 45.5 x 61.0 cm.
C-P683F44:M5F4M7/f-1 no. 2

345. New music. Rodolfo Guzmán. Nov. 19, 1978, University of Miami, Gusman Concert Hall. [Artist]: Arturo. [Miami, Fla., 1978].
B&w; 45.7 x 28.0 cm.
C-P683F44:M5C8C613/f-1 no. 4

346. A new voice for Florida. Vote Raúl Pozo for state representative. District 110. Republican Pd. Pol. Ad. Paid for by N. Drake, treasurer. [Miami, Fla., n.d.]
Color; 55.2 x 35.5 cm.
C-P683F44:M5P513H68/f-1 no. 6

347. New World Center Campus, annual student art exhibition, April 22 to May 21, 1982. Opening reception, April 22... Frances Wolfson Art Gallery... Poster design by Juan Carlos García, class of 1982. [Miami, Fla.] : Miami Dade Community College, 1982.
Color; 41.0 x 26.2 cm.
C-P683F44:M5C8A713/f-1 no. 7

348. 1985. March, Sunday 3. Paseo at downtown. The Kiwanis Club of Little Havana invites you to 10th best Calle Ocho Festival ever.. Carnaval Night at Orange Bowl, Saturday 2. [Designed by]: Rubén Travieso. [Miami, Fla.], : The Miami Herald Pub. Co., 1985.
Color; 45.0 x 55.5 cm.
C-P683F44:M5F4C3/f-3 no. 28

349. Un niño de su cariño me dio un beso tan sincero, que al morir si acaso muero, sentiré el beso del niño, José Martí. Reproduction of revista _Areíto_, Año II, number 4, Primavera 1976... [Chicago, Ill.: Abdala Chicago Delegation, 1976].
Sepia; 39 x 44 cm.
C87-2-PO-12

350. Nissan Grand Prix of Miami. April 6-7, 1991. IMSA, Good Year, RC Cola, Bud Light, Love 94, Ryder System, South Florida Nissan Dealers, 4 WTVJ, Nissan, Perry Ellis, Camel GT, Amoco, Continental. [Miami, Fla.], 1991.
Color; 78.6 x 69.5 cm.
C-P683F44:M5G7/f-2 no. 11

351. Nissan Grand Prix of Miami, for the Camel GT Championship February 24-25, 1990... [Miami, Fla.], 1990.
Color; 71.5 x 56.6 cm.
C-P683F44:M5G7/f-1 no. 10

352. Nissan Grand Prix of Miami, presented by Xtra Super Food Centers. March 4-5, 1989. Lasercolor art by: Bill Stohl... [Miami, Fla.], 1989.
Color; 58.2 x 86.4 cm.
C-P683F44:M5G7/f-1 no. 8

353. Nissan Indy Challenge at Tamiami Park, Miami, Florida. Nov, 4, 5, 6, 1988. _The Miami Herald_, Vivitar, Haagen-Dazs, Thrifty Car Rental. CART/PPG Indy Car World Series.: Lasercolor art by: Bill Stohl. [Miami, Fla.] : Championship Auto Racing Teams, Inc., 1988.
Color; 43.2 x 61.0 cm.

62

C-P683F44:M5I5/f-1 no. 4

354. Nissan Indy Challenge. Cart/PPG Indy Car World Series.
     Friday, October 30, 1987-Sunday, November 1, 1987...
     Official sponsors: Nissan, Eastern, *The Miami Herald*,
     Mobil, Rose Auto Stores, Goodyear, Miller High Life,
     Domino's Pizza, Marlboro, Mobile Vision. Lasercolor art
     by: Bill Stohl. [Miami, Fla.?: Championship Auto Racing
     Teams, Inc.], 1987.
     Color; 62.1 x 86.5 cm.
     C-P683F44:M5I5/f-1 no. 3

355. Nissan Indy Challenge, November 7, 8, 9, 1986. Cart/PPG
     Indy Car World Series. November 7, 8, 9, 1986... Hertz,
     Wendy's, *The Miami Herald*, Surreys, Goodyear, WINZ 95,
     Nissan, Stroh's, Rose Auto Stores, Eastern, Pepsi-Cola,
     7Up. [Miami, Fla.?] : Championship Auto Racing Teams,
     Inc.], 1986.
     Color; 60.0 x 84.5 cm.
     C-P683F44:M5I5/f-1 no. 2

356. ¡No podemos esperar por la OEA ni por las democracias...
     Ingresemos en alguna agrupación y podremos hacerlo muy
     pronto! Nacionalismo Realista. Nosotros lo haremos... Si
     Fidel no le temiera a la organización del exilio, no
     hubiera enviado para acá los 5000 agentes comunistas que
     informó el FBI. Cubano: de las 168 horas que tiene la
     semana, dale aunque sea 2 a tu patria. Ingresa en alguna
     agrupación. [Miami, Fla., Nacionalismo Realista, 196-?]
     B&w; 21.6 x 35.5 cm.
     C-P683F44:M5A513/f-1 no. 6

357. IX Feria Nacional Municipios de Cuba en el Exilio. Abril 4
     al 7 1991. Flagler Dog Track... Miami, Florida. Budweiser
     King of Beers. Bailes cubanos típicos: Carnaval Colonial.
     [Artist] : Mattias 1991. Goya, *El Nuevo Herald*, Radio
     Mambi WAQI 710 AM, WLTV 23, W-QBA 1140 AM La Cubanísima.
     [Miami, Fla.], 1991.
     Color; 40.7 x 53.1 cm.
     C-P683F44:M5F4M7/f-1 no. 8

358. 95% del pueblo cubano en contra... Nacionalismo Realista.
     Nosotros lo haremos. Escuche a las 6:30 p.m. el Noticiero
     Realista por la WMIE... [Miami, Fla.: Nacionalismo
     Realista, n.d.]
     B&w; 35.5 x 21.5 cm.
     C-P683F44:M5R313/f-1 no. 3

359. Ochún Obbayeye. Presentado por Alberto Morgan & A-1
     Productions. Dade County Auditorium. Agosto 20, 21.
     Agosto 26, 27. [Miami, Fla., 198-?]

Color; 66.3 x 43.0 cm.
C-P683F44:M5F613/f-1 no. 5

360. VIII Feria Nacional Municipios de Cuba en el Exilio. Abril
5 al 8, 1990. Flagler Dog Track...Miami, Florida.
[Drawing of]: Bailes típicos Cubanos: La Danza Cubana de
salón. Municipios en el exilio... [Miami, Fla.], 1990.
Color; 48.5 x 35.5 cm.
C-P683F44:M5F4M7/f-1 no. 7

361. Octubre 10, 1977. Federación de Estudiantes Cubanos,
Miami-Dade Community College. North Campus... [Artist]:
Judith Acosta. [Miami, Fla.], 1977.
B&w; 27.9 x 43 cm.
C87-2-PO-18

362. Octubre 10, 1868. Federación de Estudiates Cubanos, Miami-
Dade Community College. North Campus... [Artist] : Judith
Acosta. [Miami, Fla., 1978?]
B&w; 43 x 28 cm.
C87-2-PO-19

363. Old Milwaukee Beer, Old Milwaukee Light, saluda al Carnaval
Miami '85. 1985. [Milwaukee, Wis.: Old Milwaukee Beer Van
Munchen and Co.], 1985.
Color; 71.0 x 50.5 cm.
C-P683F44:M5F4C3/f-5 no. 45

364. XI Aniversario Revista Ideal. Octubre 17, domingo 3 P.M.,
Dade County Auditorium... Rolando Ochoa, Marta Pérez,
Armando Pico. Cante con los artistas en una tarde
inolvidable junto a Ideal, una revista cristiana... y
cubana! [Miami, Fla.] : Revista Ideal, [1982].
B&W; 56.0 x 43.2 cm.
C-P683F44:M5A3813/f-1 no. 1

365. Open house Calle Ocho. Bacardí Rum celebrates Calle Ocho
'89. Bacardí is a registered trademark of Bacardí &
Company limited. [Artist]: Haydee Scull, Mike Scull,
Sahara Scull. [Miami, Fla.: Bacardí Imports, Inc.], 1989.
Color; 59.5 x 45.5 cm.
C-P683F44:M5F4C3/f-6 no. 56

366. Padre Félix Varela, Cuban philosopher, patriot, priest
(1788-1853). November 4, 1988, 1:30-6:00 p.m. Mumford
Room 6th floor, James Madison Memorial Building, Library of
Congress. Luis E. Aguilar, Alberto Cordero, Felipe J.
Estévez, José M. Hernández, Antonio Hernández Travieso,
José I. Lasaga, Enrico M. Santí. Sponsored by the Hispanic
Division of the Library of Congress and the Spanish
Department, Georgetown University. [Washington, D.C.:

Library of Congress], 1988.
Color; 56.0 x 42.5 cm.
C-P683D54:R5C313V3/f-1 no. 1

367. "Padre Nuestro: ayuda a Cuba! No permitas que siga
derramando su sangre inocente!" 25 Aniversario Añorada
Cuba, diciembre 30, 8:00 p.m. Dade County Auditorium...
J. Peña, 1987. WQBA, "S" printing, Super Q, *Diario Las
Américas*, Sazón Goya, WLTV Lo Nuestro. 25 aniversario.
[Miami, Fla., 1987].
Color; 46.5 x 62.1 cm.
C-P693F44:M5S413A5/f-1 no. 5

368. "Padre nuestro, ayuda a Cuba! No permitas que siga
derramando su sangre inocente!" 25 aniversario Añorada
Cuba, diciembre 30, 8:00 p.m. Dade County Auditorium...
J. Peña, 1987. [Miami, Fla.], 1987.
Color; 62.0 x 46.5 cm.
C-P683F44:M5S413A5/f-1 no. 1

369. Paella '84. October 11, 1984. Hispanic Heritage Festival,
Miami-Dade Community College, Mitchell Wolfson New World
Center Campus... [Miami, Fla.] : Ortega Valencia, 1984.
Color; 73.0 x 34.9 cm.
C-P683F44:M5F4H5P3/f-1 no. 3

370. Paella 85. WLTV 23. Hispanic Heritage Festival, Miami,
Florida. Miami-Dade Community College, Mitchell Wolfson
New World Center Campus... [Miami, Fla.], 1985.
Color; 86.2 x 55.6 cm.
C-P683F44:M5F4H5P3/f-1 no. 2

371. Paella '88. October 8, 1988. Miami-Dade Community
College. Wolfson Campus. Christopher Columbus
Quincentenary Jubilee Commission... [Miami, Fla.], 1988.
Color; 71.5 x 45.7 cm.
C-P683F44:M5F4H5P3/f-1 no. 4

372. Paella '89. Saturday, October 14, 1989. Miami Dade
Community College, Wolfson Campus. Christopher Columbus
500 Quincentenary Jubilee Commission. Design by Pierre
Pierson. [Miami, Fla.], 1989.
Color; 73.0 x 46.0 cm.
C-P683F44:M5F4H5P3/f-1 no. 5

373. The Panovs Valery & Galina. Presented by Ballet Concerto
Co... Full orchestra conductor: Alfredo Munar... Costume
designer: Antonio. Dade County Auditorium, Sunday, April
22, 1979. 7:30 p.m. [Miami, Fla.], 1979.
Sepia; 63.2 x 45.5 cm.
C-P683F44:M5C8B313/f-1 no. 2

378. La Parada de los Reyes Magos. Artist: Aldo Amador. Miami, Fla., 1986.

374. The Panovs Valery & Galina. Presented by Ballet Concerto
     Co... Full orchestra conductor: Paul Csonka. Costume
     designer: Antonio, July 7, 8:15 p.m. Dade County
     Auditorium. Poster designed by Arsenio. [Miami, Fla., n.d.]
     Color; 86.2 x 34.2 cm.
     C-P683F44:M5C8B313/f-1 no. 1

375. Para acabar con la tiranía, hay que matar al tirano.
     [Miami, Fla., n.d.]
     B&w; 47.4 x 33.0 cm.
     C-P683F44:M5L45C8/f-1 no. 5

376. ¡Para Cuba es hora ya! Gran marcha por la liberación de
     Cuba. Domingo 28 de enero a la 1:00 P.M. Salida del
     parque Muñoz Rivera Puerta de Tierra. Hermano
     puertorriqueño, únete a este clamor de libertad. [San
     Juan, P.R.: Marcha por la Liberación de Cuba, 1990].
     Color; 61.0 x 45.6 cm.
     C-P633P81:L45C8M3/f-1 no. 1

377. "Para Cuba que sufre...: José Martí. Tampa, 26 de noviembre
     de 1981. Un regalo del Canal 51 y Pepsi-Cola de Miami.
     Valerio 86. Edición limitada. [Miami, Fla.], 1986.
     Color; 56.0 x 43.4 cm.
     C-P683F44:M5A713V3/f-1 no. 1

378. La Parada de los Reyes Magos. 12 de enero, 1986. WQBA.
     1140 kcs. La Cubanísima. City of Miami. [Artist] : Aldo
     Amador. [Miami, Fla.], 1986.
     Color; 62.3 x 44.0 cm.
     C-P683F44:M5P213T3/f-1 no. 2

379. La Parroquia de San Juan Bosco presenta: La Pasión de
     Cristo. Dirección: Antonio Losada. Escenografía:
     Demetrio. Actuación como Jesús: Benjamín Marcos. Dade
     County Auditorium, abril 12, 1981 (domingo)... Miami,
     Fla.: "S" Printing, [1981].
     Color; 43.8 x 28.0 cm.
     C-P683F44:M5R6P3/f-1 no. 1

380. Participa, Congreso Int'l de Jóvenes Cubanos por una Cuba
     libre. Agosto 31/Sept. 2, 1990. Hotel Eden Roc... Miami
     Beach, Florida... [Miami, Fla.], 1990.
     Color; 43.0 x 28.0 cm.
     C-P683F44:M5C8C713/f-1 no. 3

381. El Patronato Cubano de Producciones Forum... presenta una
     nueva versión de "La gentil de ayer," zarzuela cubana del
     mtro. Luis Carballo... Cuerpo de baile de Ballet Concerto.
     Dirección René Alejandro. Abril 7 y 8, 1979, Centro
     Comunitario de la Pequeña Habana. [Artist] : María A.

Madruga. [Miami, Fla.], 1979.
B&w; 43.0 x 27.5 cm.
C-P683F44:M5C8Z313/f-1 no. 2

382. Patronato del Teatro Las Máscaras presenta "Don Juan
Tenorio" de José Zorilla. Dade County Auditorium, domingo
5 de nov. única presentación. Con: Salvador Ugarte, Aurora
Collazo [et al]. Dirección Carlos Badías... [Miami, Fla.:
Patronato del Teatro Las Máscaras, n.d.]
Color; 53.5 x 41.2 cm.
C-P683F44:M5T513M3/f-1 no. 5

383. Patronato del Teatro "Las Máscaras" presenta la inolvidable
comedia de los hnos. Alvares Quintero "Malvaloca". Con
toda la gracia y el salero de Sevilla... Dade County
Auditorium, domingo, 8 de abril... [Miami, Fla.: Patronato
del Teatro Las Máscaras, n.d.]
Color; 42.0 x 27.8 cm.
C-P683F44:M5T513M3/f-1 no. 2

384. Pepsi celebra el 20 de mayo. [Artist]: Luis Vega. [Miami,
Fla.], 1987.
Color; 82.0 x 57.5 cm.
C-P683F44:M5A3813V4/f-1 no. 2

385. Pepsi le invita a participar en la piñata ¡más grande del
mundo! Certificada por los jueces del Guiness Book of
World Records. Calle Ocho, domingo, marzo 11... para niños
de 4 a 10 años... West New York, N.J.: Promotions and
Advertising Group, n.d.
Color; 65.0 x 51.0 cm.
C-P683F44:M5F4C3/f-7 no. 61

386. Personajes de Rodón. Alicia Alonso. Museo de Arte de
Ponce, 6 de abril-4 de junio de 1984. Exposición organizada
por el recinto de Rio Piedras, con motivo del octagésimo
aniversario de la Universidad de Puerto Rico. Foto: Jesús
E. Marrero. Diseño: Francisco J. Barrenchea. Francisco
Rodón, 1984. Con el auspicio de Becker Paribas. [Río
Piedras, P.R.: Univ. de Puerto Rico], 1984.
Color; 91.5 x 61.0 cm.
C-P633P81:C8A713/f-1 no. 2

387. Piedra. Exposición. Galería El Morro. San Juan, octubre
31-69. Piedra. [San Juan, P.R.], 1969.
Color; 45.7 x 26.7 cm.
C-P633P81:C8A713/f-1 no. 1

388. Polar. Domingo marzo 13 en la Calle Ocho y S.W. 16th Ave.
La orquesta de Venezuela Los Guaco y Miami Merengue.
Cerveza Polar importada. Bienvenidos al Festival de la

Calle Ocho!   Hialeah, Fla. : Screen Printing Industries,
Inc. [n.d.]
Color; 44.5 x 58.5 cm
C-P683F44:M5F4C3/f-5 no. 43

389.   Polles.   September 8-October 9, 1987.   Cuban Museum of Arts
and Culture... [Miami, Fla.], 1987.
Color; 84.4 x 43.7 cm.
C-P683F44:M5M813M8/f-1 no. 4

390.   Por primera vez alguien ha demostrado con hechos que usted
puede ser muy feliz.   Felicidad en la tierra: ¡A pesar de
todo!   Amar para vivir [by] Daniel Román... Ambas obras,
publicadas por Ediciones 29 de Barcelona. [Miami, Fla.?
n.d.]
B&w; 43.1 x 27.0 cm.
C-P683F44:M5M413B6/f-1 no. 5

391.   Pottery Questions II an exhibition of contemporary
ceramics. William Daley, James Makins, Ruth Duckworth,
Pablo Picasso, Robert Turner, February 2-25, 1985, Broward
Community College. March 8-April 9, 1985 Bacardí Art
Gallery. Poster designed by Juan Espinosa. [Miami, Fla.] :
Printed by Modern Printing, Inc., [1985.]
Color; 45/5 x 61.0 cm.
C-P683F44:M5C8A7B3/f-1 no. 2

392.   Presentación única de Libertad Lamarque.   Dade County
Auditorium... Agosto, sábado 6, domingo 7.   Maestro
Alfredo Malerba, director musical.   Manolo de Cañal,
productor general... [Miami, Fla., n.d.]
Color; 56.8 x 43.5 cm.
C-P683F44:M5C8C611/f-1 no. 1

393.   Presented by the Association of Hispanic Arts, Inc.
Exhibition. Imna Arroyo, Renán Darío Arango, [et al].
Hispanic artists in New York. City Gallery... New York,
August 10-September 4, 1981... Design: Ana and Jorge
Hernández. [New York: Association of Hispanic Arts, Inc.,
1981].
Color; 54.0 x 43.5 cm.
C-P683N74:N4A76/f-1 no. 4

394.   1er Festival SEA presentado por la Asociación de Arte y
Cultura Latinoamericana y el professor Carlos Canet.
Santería, espiritismo, astrología. "Abakua"... Lugar:
Milander Auditorium. Fecha: domingo 8 de diciembre de
1985. [Miami, Fla.] : Colorama Printing, 1985.
Color; 43.0 x 28.0 cm.
C-P683F44:M5F613/f-1 no. 4

395. Pro Arte Grateli celebra su duodécimo aniversario dedicando
     estas funciones al *Diario Las Américas* en su vigésimo-
     séptimo aniversario. Presenta a Blanca Varela, Rafael
     Lebrón en María la O... Dirección musical: mtro. Alfredo
     Munar. Dirección coral: Marta Pérez. Coreografía: Gustavo
     Roig... Asistente de dirección: Eugenio Ramos. Dirección
     artística y actuación: Miguel de Grandy II. Dade County
     Auditorium, julio 27 (domingo). Productores: Marta Pérez,
     Pili de la Rosa, Demetrio. [Miami, Fla., 1980].
     B&w; 48.0 x 29.5 cm.
     C-P683F44:M5C8Z313/f-1 no. 3

396. Pro Arte Grateli presenta a Juan Luis Galiardo el gran
     actor español triunfador de la telenovela Colorina, en la
     simpatiquísima comedia Feliz cumpleaños... Poster y
     portada: Adelfa Cantelli. Fotos: Asela. Dade County
     Auditorium, agosto 28, Miami, Florida, 1983. [Miami,
     Fla.]: Estudio Cantelli [1983].
     B&w; 33.0 x 21.5 cm.
     C-P683F44:M5T513P7/f-1 no. 1

397. Pro Arte Grateli presenta Mariano Mores y su espectacular
     show latinoamericano. Héctor Gagliardi el poeta de Buenos
     Aires, Claudia Mores, Victor Ayos y su ballet, Nito Mores.
     Dade County Auditorium, octubre 23, 1982. Productores:
     Marta Pérez, Pili de la Rosa, Demetrio. [Miami, Fla.] :
     Estudio Cantelli, 1982.
     B&w; 55.6 x 38.0 cm.
     C-P683F44:M5C8M805/f-1 no. 1

398. Pro Arte Grateli presents gala evening honoring the famous
     Cuban conductor Alberto Bolet on his 50th Anniversary. As
     conductor featuring Jorge Bolet guest of honor. Teresa
     Escandón, pianist and the University of Miami Symphony
     Orchestra... Dade County Auditorium. Saturday, November 22.
     Producers: Marta Pérez, Pili de la Rosa, Demetrio. [Miami,
     Fla., n.d.]
     B&w; 35.5 x 21.5 cm.
     C-P683F44:M5H513/f-1 no. 2

399. Pro Arte Grateli y Enrique Beltrán, Carrusel, presentan el
     acontecimiento teatral del añó, "La Fierecilla domada" de
     William Shakespeare... Dirección: Mario Martín. Dirección
     musical: Marta Pérez. Vestuario: Antonio. Escenografía y
     luces: Antonio y Demetrio. Sábado 26 de septiembre, Dade
     County Auditorium. Productores de Pro Arte Grateli: Marta
     Pérez, Pili de la Rosa, Demetrio... Poster patrocinado por:
     "Teatro Marti" y "La Comedia." [Miami, Fla., n.d.]
     B&w; 50.5 x 35.0 cm.
     C-P683F44:M5T513P7/f-1 no. 2

403. Pro Arte Lírico presenta la zarzuela Cecilia
Valdés del maestro Gonzalo Roig. Designed by
Rogelio Zelada. San Juan, P.R., n.d.

400. Pro Arte Grateli y Orfeo Elete presentan a Mara González y
Sergio Doré, hijo, en el estreno en Norteamérica de El
Barberillo de Lavapiés, zarzuela del maestro F.A.
Barbieri... Dade County Auditorium, sábado 24 de mayo,
domingo 25 de mayo. Dirección musical: mtro. Alfredo
Munar. Dirección artística: René Alejandro. Dirección
coral: Caruch Rumbaut... Esta presentación forma parte del
Primer Festival Hispano de Teatro organizado por Acting
Together. [Miami, Fla. 1986].
B&w; 57.0 x 44.2 cm.
C-P683F44:M5C8Z3/f-1 no. 2

401. Pro Arte Grateli y WLTV 23 presentan un evento para la
historia. Festival Ernesto Lecuona. La música de sus
zarzuelas, operetas y revistas, julio 26, 1986, Dade County
Auditorium... Actuaciones especiales de Blanca Varela y
directamente desde Nueva York, la presentación por primera
vez en Grateli de: América Crespo. Maestros de ceremonia:
Mara y Orlando... Estas presentaciones están dedicadas al
Diario Las Américas en su XXXIV aniversario. Productores y
directores de la Sociedad Pro Arte Grateli: Marta Pérez,
Pili de la Rosa, Demetrio. [Miami, Fla.], 1986.
B&w; 38.7 x 32.0 cm.
C-P683F44:M5F4M813E7/f-1 no. 1

402. Pro Arte Lírico presenta al estreno en Puerto Rico de María
La O de Ernesto Lecuona. Centro de Bellas Artes, Sala
Paoli... Enero 20, 8:30 P.M Gala premier auspiciada por
Hogar Sor María. Enero 21, 8:30 P.M. Enero 22, 3:30
P.M... Proyecto auspiciado por el Instituto de Cultura
Puertorriqueña y la Fundación Nacional de las Artes. [San
Juan, P.R., n.d.]
Color; 56.5 x 40.5 cm.
C-P633P81:C8Z313/f-1 no. 1

403. Pro Arte Lírico presenta la zarzuela Cecilia Valdés del
maestro Gonzalo Roig. Centro de Bellas Artes, agosto 9-10,
17, 8:30 p.m., agosto 11, 18, 3:30 p.m... Diseño: Rogelio
Zelada. [San Juan, P.R., n.d.]
Color; 55.7 x 40.5 cm.
C-P683F44:M5C8Z313/f-1 no. 4

404. Proctor & Gamble con Universal Studios Hollywood les
brindan un carnaval de premios y ahorros... Con las super
estrellas Menudo, Franco, Belkis Concepción, domingo, 13 de
marzo, calle 8... compartiendo una tradición familiar.
Foto de Cancún cortesía de Fonatur. [Miami, Fla., n.d.]
Color; 58.7 x 45.7 cm.
C-P683F44:M5F4C3/f-5 no. 42

405. Procter and Gamble con Universal Studios Hollywood les

brindan un Carnaval de premios y ahorros... ¡Venga a divertirse en la Calle Ocho en el supersite de Proctor and Gamble... Domingo, 13 de marzo. Calle 8 y Avenida 22 del S.W... [Miami, Fla., n.d.]
Color; 58.6 x 45.6 cm.
C-P683F44:M5F4C3/f-6 no. 53

406. Producciones Forum y Producciones ALAFI presentan a Virginia Alonso y Armando Rodríguez en Los Gavilanes, zarzuela del maestro José Serrano... Desde abril 29 hasta mayo 14, Teatro América. [Artist]: Nena. [Miami, Fla., n.d.]
B&w; 43.0 x 28.0 cm.
C-P683F44:M5C8Z3/f-1 no. 1

407. Producciones M.C.T. y Teltac, S.A. presentan la 1ra. superproducción ecuatoriana con: Trespatines, Leopoldo Fernández y Evaristo, Ernesto Albán, Misión 3K3, Atlantic y Trail, Sep. 26. Vilma Carbia, Gladys Núñez, Rolando Ochoa, Mayín Fernández... Dirigida por Manny San Fernando y Leopoldo Fernández, Jr. Escrita por José A. Prieto... Productor ejecutivo: Danilo Bardisa... [Artist] : Roblán. [Miami, Fla.] : J.B. Graphics, Inc., 1980.
Color; 88.0 x 58.0 cm.
C-P683F44:M5S413M6/f-1 no. 2

408. Programa Ballet Concerto. Bailes, exposición de arte, estampas dramáticas. Semana Cubana, enero 27-28-29. Hora: 7:00 p.m. Miami Dade College - North Campus. [Miami, Fla., n.d.]
B&w; 28.0 x 43.0 cm.
C-P683F44:M5C8B313/f-1 no. 7

409. Prolírica presenta: "Los Claveles" y "Romanzas y dúos de zarzuelas". Domingos 1ro, 8, 15, y 22 de noviembre, 6:00 p.m. Teatro Bellas Artes... [Artist]: Alsar. [Miami, Fla.], 1987.
Sepia; 35.5 x 21.7 cm.
C-P683F44:M5C8Z3/f-1 no. 6

410. Prometeo-Miami Dade Community College. Estampas de la novelística cubana. Marzo 8, 1975, DC Auditorium. [Miami, Fla., 1975].
Sepia; 27.8 x 27.8 cm.
C-P683F44:M5C8P613/f-1 no. 1

411. Prometeo. Miami-Dade Community College. Mitchell Wolfson New World Center Campus, presenta octubre 26, 27, 28... Yoti Machado, José Valera, Fermín Rojas [et al]... De: Ana Bonacci, La Hora de la fantasía. Dirección: Teresa María Rojas. [Artist] : Arditti. [Miami, Fla., n.d.]

Color; 35.5 x 21.6 cm.
C-P683F44:M5T613P7/f-1 no. 2

412. El pueblo polaco ha dicho basta ya a la dictadura
comunista... únete! En respaldo al "Dia de lucha nacional"
en Polonia. Protesta este 10 de noviembre, 1982, 6 p.m.
27 Ave. del S.W. y 8 calle. [Miami, Fla.?], 1982.
B&w; 42.6 x 27.6 cm.
C87-2-PO-35

413. Punch #84. Kennedy for Congress... Pd. Pol. Adv. Democrat
Congressional District 18 Gerald Silverman, Treas. [Miami,
Fla., 1989].
Color; 33.6 x 34.6 cm.
C-P683F44:M5P513H69/f-1 no. 5

414. ¡Qué libro colosal! Apuntes para la historia, Enrique C.
Betancourt. 50 años de farándula cubana, radio, televisión
y farándula de la Cuba de ayer. Diseño: Rogelio Zelada.
[San Juan, P.R.]: Impreso en Puerto Rico por Ramallo Bros.
Printing Inc... [1986].
Color; 65.5 x 50.2 cm.
C-P633P81:M413B6/f-1 no. 1

415. 5a Feria Nacional de los Municipios de Cuba en el Exilio.
Abril 9-10, 1987. Flagler Dog Track. [Miami, Fla.], 1987.
Color; 56.0 x 35.5 cm.
C-P683F44:M5F4M7/f-1 no. 5

416. 5 Congreso de Intelectuales Cubanos Disidentes, Caracas,
Venezuela, 4, 5 y 6, septiembre '87. [Caracas], 1987.
Color; 19.3 x 116 cm.
C-P683F44:M5C8C713I5/f-1 no. 2

417. V Congreso de Intelectuales Cubanos Disidentes, Caracas,
Venezuela, 3, 4, 5 y 6, septiembre '87. [Caracas], 1987.
Color; 19.4 x 116.0 cm.
C-P683F44:M5C8C713I5/f-1 no. 1

418. Rai-Guede Films Inc. Presenta La Otra Cuba. Un film de
Orlando Jiménez-Leal... Producción: Luis Argueta. Edición:
Gloria Piñeyro. [Miami, Fla., 1990].
Color; 46.6 x 69 cm.
C-P683F44:M5F513/f-1 no. 3

419. Rai-Guede Films Inc. presents "The Other Cuba," a film by
Orlando Jiménez Leal... Producer: Luis Argueta. Editor:
Gloria Piñeyro. Adrián. [Miami, Fla., 1990].
Color; 69.5 x 46.5 cm.
C-P683F44:M5F513C2/f-1 no. 2

427. Re-Encuentro Cubano 1977. Artist: Lezcano.
Miami, Fla., 1977.

420. Ralph Mercado presenta el Festival de Salsa part 1 en Nueva
York, Sat. Sept. 2. Celia Cruz, El Gran Combo... 7 P.M.
show... Forest Hills Tennis Stadium, Queens, N.Y. [New
York, n.d.]
Color; 73.3 x 38.3 cm.
C-P683N74:N4F313/f-1 no. 1

421. The Ramiro Fernández Collection. Salon and Picturesque
Photography in Cuba 1860-1920... October 5 to January 14.
Historical Museum of Southern Florida. This exhibit is
made possible through the generous support of Southeast
Banking Corporation Foundation, the South Florida Cultural
Consortium, and the Metro-Dade Cultural Affairs Council,
Tourist Tax Program. Endorsed by the Hispanic Heritage
Festival of Miami, Florida. [Miami, Fla.] : Historical
Museum of Southern Florida, [1989].
B&w; 93.5 x 66.0 cm.
C-P683F44:M5P3R3/f-1 no. 1

422. Recital (experimento poético-musical sobre texto de José
Mario). Mayté Criado y José Mario, 25 de junio, 1981, a
las 20 horas... junio 1981. Galería de Arte Zodíaco, José
Ortega y Gasset, 23. [Madrid] : Ediciones La Gota de Agua,
1981.
Color; 45.0 x 33.0 cm.
C-P683F44:M5C8P613/f-1 no. 2

423. Recordando los carnavales de Santiago de Cuba en Tropical
Park 28 de abril de 1990, 7:00 p.m. a 1:00 a.m...
[Patronicadores]: Metro-Dade, WLTV 23... [Miami, Fla.],
1990.
Color; 73.5 x 58.5 cm.
C-P683F44:M5F4C2413/f-1 no. 1

424. Recuerde, cante, ría, compruebe que cualquier tiempo pasado
fue mejor con Mara y Orlando, los artistas creadores de los
festivales que han conquistado el corazón de Miami...
Domingo 21 de febrero, 3:00 p.m... Dade County Auditorium.
[Miami, Fla., n.d.]
B&w; 35.5 x 21.6 cm.
C-P683F44:M5C8C613/f-2 no. 20

425. Re-elect Durán Councilman. Pd. pol. adv. [Miami, Fla.,
n.d.]
Color; 45.6 x 15.3 cm.
C-P683F44:M5P513C44/f-1 no. 1

426. Re-elect Javier Souto state senator. Pd. Pol. Adv. by
Javier Souto Campaign. Rep. Dist. 40. [Miami, Fla.] :
Tim-Cor Poly-art, [1990].
Color; 56.0 x 35.5 cm.

C-P683F44:M5P513S48/f-1 no. 4

427. Re-Encuentro Cubano 1977, junio 24-junio 30. Exhibición de
pintura y escultura. Concierto sinfónico. Obra teatral.
Dibujos humorísticos. Eventos populares. Auspiciado por:
National Endowment for the Arts, City of Miami, University
of Miami, Comité Comunitario. [Artist] : Lezcano. Limited
48/100. [Miami, Fla.], 1977.
Silkscreen, Color; 75.0 x 38.0 cm.
C-P683F44:M5C8C713R4/f-1 no. 1

428. Reinol González, y Fidel creó el punto X. Un testimonio
revelador sobre el régimen de Castro. Saeta Ediciones. De
venta aquí. [Miami, Fla., 1988].
Color; 46.0 x 31.9 cm.
C-P683F44:M5M413B6/f-1 no. 6

429. Representative Javier Souto for state senator. Pd. Pol.
Adv. District 40. [Miami, Fla., 1988].
Color; 43.0 x 27.8 cm.
C-P683F44:M5P513S48/f-1 no. 2

430. Rescatemos al Museo Cubano del comercio con Castro.
Adhesiones al Comité Pro-rescate al Museo Cubano... [Miami,
Fla.: Comité Pro-rescate Museo Cubano, 1988].
B&w; 71.0 x 45.6 cm.
C-P683F44:M5M813M8/f-1 no. 6

431. Rescue the Cuban Museum. Limited Edition 67/150. [Miami,
Fla.: Cuban Museum Rescue Committe], 1988. Autographed by
artists.
Color; 55.4 x 87.8 cm
C-P683F44:M5M813M8/f-1 no. 7

432. Ricardo Núñez for Congress. Authorized and paid for by
Ricardo Núñez for Congress Committe/ Leonardo Gravier, CPA,
Treasurer/Republican 744. [Miami, Fla., n.d.]
Color; 35.5 x 71.0 cm.
C-P683F44:M5P513H69/f-1 no. 1

433. Roberto Martín Pérez. Es el preso político cubano más
antiguo del continente. [Artist]: Kadava Jo--? 10-13-77
[Miami, Fla.] : Comité Pro-Libertad de Roberto Martín
Pérez, [1977].
B&w; 44.3 x 29.0 c.m.
C-P683F44:M5P6613C8/f-1 no. 1

434. The Romantic East, a one man show of paintings by Murray
Gaby. The Bacardí Art Gallery from April 5th through April
23rd, 1971. [Miami, Fla.: Bacardí Imports, Inc.], 1971.
Color; 55.8 x 43.0 cm.

C-P683F44:M5C8A7B3/f-2 no. 13

435. Ros-Lehtinen, Congress. Paid by Ros Lehtinen for Congress
Committee-Rep. Miami, Fla.: Allied Printing, [1989].
Color; 35.5 x 56.0 cm.
C-P683F44:M5P513H69/f-1 no. 2

436. Rosario Hiriart, Nuevo espejo de paciencia. Ediciones
Caballo Griego para la Poesía, Madrid, España. Breve
novela... [Artist]: Mano Boj. Miami, Fla.: Ediciones
Universal, 1988.
Color; 43.0 x 35.5 cm.
C-P683F44:M5M413B6/f-1 no. 7

437. St. John Bosco Church VI Festival de Otoño. Sunshine
Amusements. Octubre 17, 18, 19, 1986... Baltimore, MD :
Globe Poster [1986].
Color; 58.7 x 35.5 cm.
C-P683F44:M5F313/f-1 no. 2

438. Sala Teatro Arlequín presenta a Virginia Rambal, Chamaco
García en Un matrimonio a la italiana. Filomena Marturano
de Eduardo di Filippo... Viernes y sábado... Sala Teatro
Arlequín. [Miami, Fla., n.d.]
B&w; 36.3 x 28.0 cm.
C-P683F44:M5T513S3/f-1 no. 1

439. Sarduy Gallery, 207 E. 85th Street, New York, N.Y.,
presents Baruj Salinas. May 5 to May 19, 1970. Preview:
May 5, 5-7 p.m. [Artist] : Baruj Salinas. [New York],
1970.
Color; 43.0 x 27.9 cm.
C-P683N74:N4C8A713/f-1 no. 1

440. Seasons Greetings from this your preferred super market and
the Cawy products family. Materva, Yerba Mate Soda.
[Artist]: Mayra. [Miami, Fla., n.d.]
Color; 54.0 x 44.0 cm.
C-P683F44:M5M413B4/f-1 no. 1

441. Second Annual Auction and exhibition, Miami Mental Health
Center. Koubek Memorial Center... Miami. April 20-25.
Auction, April 26, at 3 P.M., 1986... Designer: Juan
Martín. [Miami, Fla.] : Credit Bank, 1986.
Color; 61.0 x 46.0 cm.
C-P683F44:M5C8A713M5/f-1 no. 1

442. 2do Congreso de Intelectuales Cubanos Disidentes. Cuba:
represión y expansión. 28-31 Agosto 1980, Teachers
College, Colombia University. Nueva York: Comité de
Intelectuales por la Libertad de Cuba, 1980.

Color; 74.5 x 59.0 cm.
C-P683F44:M5C8C713I5/f-1 no. 4

443. 2do. Congreso Nacional Abdala, agosto 3-6. [Miami, Fla., 1972?]
Color; 91 x 60 cm.
C87-2-PO-4

444. II Festival de Teatro Hispano... 1-31 de Mayo de 1987... presentado por: Acting Together, Inc. [Artist]: Aldo Amador. Poster design: Fausto Sánchez, [Miami]: Sánchez & Levitán Advertising, Inc., 1987.
Color; 61.0 x 36.2 cm.
C-P683F44:M5F4H6/f-1 no. 4

445. VII Feria Nacional, Municipios de Cuba en el Exilio. Abril 6/9, 1989. Flagler Dog Track... [Artist]: Matias. Bailes típicos cubanos "Zapateo Criollo". [Miami, Fla.], 1989.
Color; 61.3 x 38.8 cm.
C-P683F44:M5F4M7/f-1 no. 6

446. 7mo Congreso Internacional Abdala, 4-7 agosto, 1977. [Artist: Luis Fernández-Puente. Miami, Fla.?, 1977].
Color; 71 x 38.5 cm.
C87-2-PO-17

447. 62 de todo un poco... 71. Ricardo Viera. Greater Fall River Art Association 80 Belmont Street, Fall River, Massachusetts. Opening: October 2, 8:00 p.m. Exhibit through October 22. [Fall River, Mass.: Greater Fall River Art Association, 1971?]
Color; 52.0 x 35.5 cm.
C-P683F44:M5C8A713/f-1 no. 5

448. Seventh Hispanic Arts Festival. A month long celebration of Hispanic dance, music, theatre and visual arts! Exhibition featuring works selected by Cayman Gallery... October 5th to 31st, 1982. Produced by the Association of Hispanic Arts, Inc... Transit Advertising paid by Chemical Bank. New York [1982].
Color; 28.0 x 71.2 cm.
C-P683N74:N4A76/f-1 no. 5

449. VI Feria Nacional de los Municipios de Cuba en el Exilio. Abril 7 al 10, 1988. Flagler Dog Track. [Artist] : Matías. [Miami, Fla.], 1988.
Color; 61.0 x 35.7 cm.
C-P683F44:M5F4M7/f-1 no. 1

450. 6to. Congreso Internacional Abdala, julio 30-agosto 1, 1976. [Artist: Luis Fernandez-Puente. Miami, Fla., 1976.]

Color; 76 x 57 cm.
C87-2-PO-13

451.   "El Show de los Grandes", a reírse con Rosendo Rosell!!!
       Domingo 15 de junio, Dade County Auditorium. Tremendo show
       de risas y canciones... Música dirigida por el maestro Tony
       Matas... Dirección general: Rosendo Rosell. [Miami, Fla.,
       198-?]
       B&w; 34.2 x 21.6 cm.
       C-P683F44:M5C8M813/f-1 no. 5

452.   "El Show de los Grandes", domingo 7 de junio 3 de la tarde.
       Dade County Auditorium... ¡A reírse con Rosendo Rosell! El
       gran comediante de América en el juguete cómico "Rosendo
       Rosell llegó del Mariel"... [Miami, Fla., 198-?]
       Color; 28.0 x 21.5 cm.
       C-P683F44:M5F4M813/f-1 no. 1

453.   Si necesitas ayuda en: matrícula, orientación, ayuda
       financiera... Federación de Estudiantes Cubanos. [Queens
       College, New York, 1967?]
       B&w; 35 x 22 cm.
       C87-2-PO-1

454.   Simposium de Teatro Latinoamericano. Prometeo en
       colaboración con la Universidad Internacional de la Florida
       presenta "La Abuela" y "El Viaje", dos obras en un acto de
       Orlando González-Esteva... Auditorium Miami-Dade Community
       College. New World Center Campus... [Miami, Fla., n.d.]
       B&w; 35.5 x 21.5 cm.
       C-P683F44:M5T613P7/f-1 no. 1

455.   6th Annual Grand Prix of Miami. For the Camel GT
       Championship. Feb. 27-28, 1988. [Miami, Fla.] : 1987.
       Color; 62.0 x 46.0 cm.
       C-P683F44:M5G7/f-1 no. 7

456.   VI International Hispanic Theatre Festival. VI Festival
       Internacional De Teatro Hispano. May 31-June 16, 1991.
       Minorca Playhouse, Coral Gables, Florida. Produced by
       Teatro Avante. [Artist] : Maria Brito. [Miami, Fla.],
       1991.
       Color; 75 x 61 cm.
       C-P683F44:M5F4H6/f-1 no. 7

457.   Sociedad Artístico-Cultural de las Américas presenta con
       orgullo la más famosa de las zarzuelas, Luisa Fernanda.
       Orquesta Sinfónica. Dirección musical: mtro. Manuel
       Ochoa.Dirección de escena: Néstor Cabell. Sábado 12 de
       abril, domingo 13 de abril. Gusman Philharmonic Hall.
       [Artist]: R. Delfín. [Miami, Fla.], 1975.

B&w; 59.0 x 44.5 cm.
C-P683F44:M5C8Z3/f-1 no. 3

458. S[ociedad] Pro Arte Grateli. Miami, Florida. [Miami, Fla., n.d.]
Color; 50.5 x 45 cm.
C-P683F44:M5T513P7/f-1 no. 3

459. Sociedad Pro Arte en su 19 aniversario dedica esta función a *Diario Las Américas* en su 34 aniversario de fundado. Presenta a Manolo Codeso, Milagros Ponti en La Rosa del azafrán... Dirección musical: mtro. Alfredo Munar. Dirección general: Manolo codeso. Dirección coral: mtro. Jesús García... [Miami, Fla., 1987].
C-P683F44:M5C8Z3/f-1 no. 4

460. Sociedad Pro Arte Grateli, Ballet Concerto. Cuban Folklore presentan Folklore Cubano... Dirección musical y orquestación: mtro. Alfredo Munar... Directores Ballet Concerto Co. y Cuban Folklore: Sonia Díaz, Martha del Pino, Eduardo Recalt, Antonio. Directores y productores de la Sociedad Pro Arte Grateli: Marta Pérez, Pili de la Rosa, Demetrio. Un evento del Carnaval Miami. Dade County Auditorium. Febrero 27 & 28. [Miami, Fla., n.d.]
B&w; 35.5 x 21.6 cm.
C-P683F44:M5F613/f-1 no. 3

461. Sociedad Pro Arte Grateli celebrando su 20 aniversario dedica esta función a *Diario Las Américas* en su 35 aniversario de fundado presenta a la bellísima zarzuela La Tabernera del puerto... Orquesta Sinfónica. Director musical: mtro. Manuel Ochoa... Flyers y portada: Adelfa Cantelli. Dade County Auditorium, julio 30-julio 31. Miami, Fla., 1988.
B&w; 36.0 x 21.4 cm.
C-P683F44:M5C8Z3/f-1 no. 5

462. Sociedad Pro Arte Grateli, *Diario Las Américas*, Miami Dance Futures presentan: Ballet Español Rosita Segovia... 11 de noviembre, Dade County Auditorium. Productores y directores de la Sociedad Pro Arte Grateli. Marta Perez, Pili de la Rosa, Demetrio. [Miami, Fla., 1990].
B&W; 21.6 x 31.6 cm.
C-P683F44:M5C8B3/f-1 no. 1

463. Sociedad Pro Arte Grateli, *Diario Las Américas*, 51 WSCV presentan: Evangelina Colón (directamente de Viena)... Actuación especial de Ballet Concerto Youth Company, Coral Grateli, Orquesta Sinfónica. Director musical: mtro Manuel Ochoa. El vestuario de Evangelina Colón es original de

Antonio... Directores y productores de la Sociedad Pro Arte Grateli: Marta Pérez, Pili de la Rosa, Demetrio. Dade County Auditorium: Octubre 29, sábado 8:15 p.m.-Octubre 30, domingo 3:15 p.m. Miami, Fla., 1988.
B&w; 34.0 x 21.5 cm.
C-P683F44:M5C8Z3/f-1 no. 7

464. La Sociedad Pro Arte Grateli, *Diario Las Américas* y WLTV Canal 23 presentan, celebrando el centenario del natalicio del maestro Gonzalo Roig su inmortal zarzuela cubana Cecilia Valdés... Dirección musical y orquestaciones: Maestro Alfredo Munar... Coordinación de vestuario femenino y afiche: Antonio... Directores y productores de La Sociedad Pro Arte Grateli: Marta Pérez, Pili de la Rosa, Demetrio. Sábado 23 de junio, 8:15 P.M. Domingo 24 de junio, 3:15 p.m. Dade County Auditorium. [Miami, Fla., 1990].
Sepia; 35.3 x 21.7 cm.
C-P683F44:M5C8Z313/f-1 no. 6

465. Sociedad Pro Arte Grateli presenta dos espectáculos extraordinarios. Historias de la música cubana, dos biografías, dos crónicas del arte cubano que conquistó el mundo creadas e interpretadas por Mara y Orlando... Como un homenaje al Presidio Político Cubano a través de los siglos. Dirección musical: Alfredo Munar... Productores y directores de la Sociedad Pro Arte Grateli: Marta Pérez, Pili de la Rosa, Demetrio. [Miami, Fla., 1988].
B&w; 38.5 x 22.1 cm.
C-P683F44:M5C8M813/f-1 no. 9

466. Sociedad Pro Arte Grateli presenta el evento del año. Festival Ernesto Lecuona 1987, una nueva versión del acontecimiento que conmovió a Miami, con la música del, extraordinario compositor... Dade County Auditorium en un espectáculo creado e interpretado por Mara y Orlando... Dirección musical: Alfredo Munar... Productores y directores de Sociedad Pro Arte Grateli: Marta Pérez, Pili de la Rosa, Demetrio. [Miami, Fla.], 1987.
Sepia; 35.5 x 21.5 cm.
C-P683F44:M5F4M813E7/f-1 no. 3

467. La Sociedad Pro Arte Grateli presenta: El Festival del Feeling. Las canciones de ayer de hoy y de siempre con el sentimiento de nuestras voces cubanas... Flyers y portada: Adelfa Cantelli. Dade County Auditorium, enero 30, sábado [Miami, Fla., n.d.]
B&w; 35.5 x 21.6 cm.
C-P683F44:M5C8M813/f-1 no. 4

468. Sociedad Pro Arte Grateli presenta un acontecimiento de

acontecimientos. Festival Ernesto Lecuona 1988. Dos
espectáculos distintos creados o interpretados por Mara y
Orlando con Zoraida Marrero, Zenaida Manfugás... Dade
County Auditorium, 20 de agosto, sábado, 8:15 p.m... la
participación especial del Dr. Ariel Remos y Jesús
Cabrisas... Dade County Auditorium 21 de agosto, domingo,
3:15 p.m. Dirección musical: mtro. Alfredo Munar...
Productores y directores de la Sociedad Pro Arte Grateli:
Marta Pérez, Pili de la Rosa, Demetrio. [Miami, Fla.],
1988.
Color; 35.5 x 21.5 cm.
C-P683F44:M5F4M813E7/f-1 no. 4

469. Sociedad Pro Arte Grateli, WLTV 23, WQBA La Cubanísima, a
petición popular presentan lo mejor del Festival Ernesto
Lecuona. Las selecciones más aplaudidas de los dos
conciertos que han conmovido a Miami, en una función
inolvidable... Un espectáculo creado, dirigido e
interpretado por Mara y Orlando. Dirección musical y
orquestaciones: Maestro Alfredo Munar... Domingo 31 de
agosto, Dade County Auditorium. [Miami, Fla., 1989?]
Sepia; 39.0 x 28.8 cm.
C-P683F44:M5F4M813E7/f-1 no. 2

470. Sociedad Pro Arte Grateli y *Diario Las Américas* lo invitan
a pasar un fin de semana inolvidable en el Festival Ernesto
Lecuona 1990. Dos espectáculos distintos creados e
interpretados por Mara y Orlando... Dade County Auditorium,
22 de Septiembre, Sábado, 8:15 P.M.; 23 de Septiembre,
domingo 3:15 P.M. Dirección musical: Alfredo Munar...
Productores y directores de la Sociedad Pro Arte Grateli:
Marta Pérez, Pili de la Rosa, Demetrio. [Miami, Fla.],
1990.
Color; 36.8 x 21.5 cm.
C-P683F44:M5F4M813E7/f-1 no. 5

471. La Sociedad Pro Arte Grateli y *Diario de las Américas*
presentan a Mara y Orlando en dos espectáculos sin
precedentes. Conozca a Cuba primero y al extranjero
despué... Primer viaje, 28 de octubre, sábado, 8:15 p.m.
Dade County Auditorium... Dirección musical: Alfredo
Munar... Productores y directores de la Sociedad Pro Arte
Grateli: Marta Pérez, Pili de la Rosa, Demetrio. [Miami,
Fla., 1991?]
Color; 36.8 x 21.5 cm.
C-P683F44:M5C8C613/f-3 no. 29

472. La Sociedad Pro Arte Grateli y *Diario Las Américas*
presentan a Olga Díaz en Navidad '89. La gran pianista
cubana nos hará viajar por el mundo con sus contagiosa
alegría a través de sus canciones, música y anécdotas. Un

regalo navideño. Dade County Auditorium. Sábado, 23 de
diciembre, 8:15 p.m... Productores y directores de la
Sociedad Pro Arte Grateli: Marta Pérez, Pili de la Rosa,
Demetrio. [Miami, Fla.], 1989.
B&w; 35.7 x 21.5 cm.
C-P683F44:M5C8C613/f-3 no. 28

473. La Sociedad Pro Arte Grateli y *Diario Las Américas*
presentan por demanda popular, directamente de New York la
genial pianista cubana Zenaida Manfugás interpretando
música de Chopin y Franz Liszt incluyendo la transcripción
de la Sinfonía (Heróica) de Beethoven... Febrero 24
(sábado), 8:15 P.M. Dade County Auditorium. Productores y
directores de la Sociedad Pro Arte Grateli: Marta Pérez,
Pili de la Rosa, Demetrio. [Miami, Fla.], 1990.
B&w; 33.0 x 21.6 cm.
C-P683F44:M5C8C613/f-3 no. 30

474. Soirée en concierto. "Llegó el momento" a beneficio de
"Amor en Acción". Dade County Auditorium. Sábado, 12 de
octubre 7:30 p.m. [Miami, Fla., n.d.]
B&W; 35.6 x 21.5 cm.
C-P683F44:M5C8C613/f-3 no. 26

475. Stroh's Beer invita a la gran fiesta de la Calle 8... Los
esperamos con Stroh's en la Calle 8, 21 y 22 Ave., domingo
6 de marzo. The official beer of the 1982 World's Fair.
Cerveza Stroh's "La nuestra". Detroit, Michigan : The Stroh
Brewery Co. [1982].
Color; 69.8 x 69.8 cm.
C-P683F44:M5F4C3/f-2 no. 20

476. The Subject is Cuba. A lecture series at Georgetown
University. November 14... Cuba y la América Latina:
Bosquejo histórico... November 21... A Round table on Cuba:
Impressions from a recent trip... December 5... Recital: La
nueva canción cubana/ the new Cuban song [Washington, D.C.,
n.d.]
Color; 43.2 x 27.9 cm.
C-P683D54:W3C68L4G4/f-1 no. 2

477. TAR presenta: Caja de sombras. Dirección: José Amaya.
Carlos Ponce, Maria Elena Sánchez Ocejo [et al]. La Danza,
sábados 12:00 p.m., domingos 9:00 p.m. [Miami, Fla., n.d.]
B&w; 42.6 x 35.8 cm.
C-P683F44:M5T513T44/f-1 no. 2

478. TH-Rodven con sus estrellas le ponen amor... y sabor a la
Calle 8 '91. TH-Rodven saluda a todos los medios de Radio
y Televsion... fm 92, Radio Ritmo, Zol stereo 98.3 FM, W-
QBA, CMQ, Telemundo, Super Q, Radio Mambí, Univisión,
485. Teatro Avante presenta el estreno mundial de
"Una Caja de Zapato Vacía." Miami, Fla., 1987.

485. Teatro Avante presenta el estreno mundial de
"Una Caja de Zapato Vacía." Miami, Fla., 1987.

Cadena Azul RHC, Radio Superior. [Miami, Fla.], 1991.
Color; 65.6 x 49.4 cm.
C-P683F44:M5F4C3/f-8 no. 75

479. TH-Rodven le pone amor y ... salsa a la Calle Ocho '90 con
sus estrellas Lalo Rodríguez, Oscar D'León, Eddie
Santiago... TH-Rodven saluda a todos los medios de radio y
televisión, responsables de hacer llegar nuestra música
todo el año al público de Miami. Design by: Drago. [Miami,
Fla.] : Artistic Designs, Inc. 1990.
Color; 65.8 x 47.0 cm.
C-P683F44:M5F4C3/f-7 no. 65

480. TH-RODVEN le pone amor y salsa al Carnaval Miami, Little
Havana U.S.A... [Miami, Fla., 1989].
Color; 56.3 x 43.6 cm.
C-P683F44:M5F4C3/f-5 no. 50

481. TH-RODVEN, Univisión, presentes en el Carnaval de Miami con
sus artistas exclusivos: Ricardo Montaner, Kiara. Véalos
en vivo en la Calle Ocho y Avenida 27 y en televisión de
costa a costa el dia 19 de marzo de 1989. [Miami, Fla.],
1989.
Color; 59.8 x 44.6 cm.
C-P683F44:M5F4C3/f-6 no. 51

482. Teatro América presenta al Centro Cultural Cubano de Nueva
York en El Super (una tragicomedia del Exilio Cubano).
Escrita y dirigida por Iván Acosta... Estreno en Miami,
jueves, viernes y sábado, 9 p.m. Teatro América. Centro
Cultural Cubano. Ilustración: Gabriel. Diseño: Torres.
[Miami, Fla] : Impresión Olmedo Printing [n.d.].
Color; 43.0 x 28.0 cm.
C-P683F44:M5T513T4/f-1 no. 2

483. Teatro Avante celebrando su primer aniversario presenta a
Teresa María Rojas, Mario Ernesto Sánchez, Alina Interián,
Julio O'Farrill en el premio Pulitzer, Un Tranvía llamado
Deseo de Tennessee Williams... Producción RAS. Desde
marzo 6 hasta abril 25. Teatro Avante. Esta presentación
"Un Tranvía llamado Deseo" está autorizada por Dramatistis
Play Service, Inc. [Miami, Fla., 1980].
B&w; 35.0 x 27.0 cm.
C-P683F44:M5T513T41/f-1 no. 2

484. Teatro Avante, Centro Cultural SIBI presentan Lorca o El
Lenguaje del amor. Espectáculo creado por Mario Ernesto
Sánchez, Rolando Moreno y René Alejandro... En el Centro
Cultural SIBI desde el 30 de noviembre hasta el 15 de
diciembre de 1985... [Miami, Fla.: SIBI], 1985.
Color; 35.5 x 21.4 cm.

C-P683F44:M5T513T41/f-1 no. 1

485. Teatro Avante presenta el estreno mundial de "Una caja de zapato vacía." de Virgilio Piñera. II Festival de Teatro Hispano de Miami. 1-10 de mayo de 1987. [Miami, Fla.], 1987.
Color; 70.5 x 40.5 cm.
C-P683F44:M5F4H6/f-1 no. 3

486. Teatro Avante presents IV Festival of Hispanic Theatre, IV Festival de Teatro Hispano. May 12-June 4, 1989. Poster design: Rolando Moreno. Minorca Playhouse, Coral Gables, Florida. [Miami, Fla., 1989].
Color; 91.5 x 62.3 cm.
C-P683F44:M5F4H6/f-1 no. 6

487. Teatro Avante, Teatro Bellas Artes. Alguna cosita que alivie el sufrir, de René R. Alomá. 2 de mayo a junio, 1986... [Miami, Fla.], 1986.
Color; 43.3 x 27.5 cm.
C-P683F44:M5F4H6/f-1 no. 2

488. Teatro Bellas Artes. Sábado 13 de abril, presenta Julián en concierto, su voz y sus canciones. Premio especial ACCA, revelación artística del año, ganador 2do lugar Festival OTI Miami... [Miami, Fla.] : Printed at AAA Printing [n.d.]
B&w 35.6 x 21.5 cm.
C-P683F44:M5C8C613/f-2 no. 13

489. Teatro Espacial No-identificado presenta: "Josefina, atiende a los señores Cuentos y cortos." Dirección: Tony Wagner, noviembre 17, 18, 24, y 25 de 1978... Una magnífica representación de cuentos y estampas de destacados escritores cubanos... [Miami, Fla.], 1978.
B&w; 35.5 x 21.6 cm.
C-P683F44:M5T513/f-1 no. 1

490. Teatro Martí #1... Changó International Productions, E. Capote y J. Martínez presentan a Jorge Martínez en "Día de fiesta." Comedia para toda la familia... [Miami, Fla., n.d.]
Color; 43.0 x 28.0 cm.
C-P683F44:M5T513T45/f-1 no. 2

491. Teatro Martí #1... Changó International Productions, E. Capote y J. Martínez presentan a Jorge Martínez en "Día de fiesta"... [Miami, Fla., n.d.]
Color; 43.0 x 28.0 cm.
C-P683F44:M5T513T45/f-1 no. 2a

492. Teatro Miami 2 presenta las estrellas del fantástico show

cómico, ¡¡Extravaganza Musical!! (Tutti Frutti Co. 2) Se reirá hasta no poder con la mejor revista cómico-musical de transformistas... Teatro Miami 2. [Miami, Fla., 1987]. B&w; 35.5 x 21.5 cm. C-P683F44:M5T513T454/f-1 no. 1

493. Teatro Miami I presenta Un Exilio de tres pares! Una comedia con chispa y humor para reír... y algo más para recordar... Diseño: Manolo de la Portilla. [Miami, Fla.] : Colorama Printing [1983]. B&w; 43.2 x 27.8 cm. C-P683F44:M5T513/f-1 no. 5

494. Teatro Para Uno y Teatro de Bellas Artes presentan la obra más violenta y controversial de nuestros tiempos, Extremos (Extremeties) de William Mastrosimone... Abril 3-26, Teatro de Bellas Artes. Esta presentación de "Extremos" está autorizada por Samuel French, Inc. [Miami, Fla., n.d.] Color; 35.7 x 21.6 cm. C-P683F44:M5T513T42/f-1 no. 2

495. Teatro Repertorio Español, productores: Gilberto Zaldívar y Mario R. Arellano y Sociedad Pro arte Grateli, productores: Marta Pérez, Pili de la Rosa, Demetrio, presentan solamente dos semanas la comedia musical Gigi... Dirección: María Julia Casanova. Dirección musical: Alfredo Munar... Teatro Repertorio Español... Diseño de poster: Arsenio. Foto: Marcel. Cortesía de Guacanayabo Motors... [Miami, Fla., n.d.] B&w; 35.5 x 21.6 cm. C-P683F44:M5T513/f-1 no. 3

496. Ten out of Cuba, a selection of Cuban artists. Juan Abreu Felippe, Carlos José Alfonso, Jaime Bellechases, Juan Boza, Pedro Damián, Víctor Gómez, Eduardo Michaelsen, José Orbein Pérez, Gilberto Ruiz, Andrés Valerio. Intar Latin American Gallery... Luis Vega. [New York: INTAR], 1982. Color; 63.7 x 44.5 cm. C-P683F44:M5C8A713/f-1 no. 10

497. "...Tengamos fe en que la razón hace la fuerza, y en esa fe, atrevámonos hasta el fin a cumplir con nuestro deber como lo entendemos"... Abraham Lincoln. O. Bosch. [Miami, Fla.?], 1977. Color; 48.3 x 71.9 cm. C-P683F44:M5A713B6/f-1 no.1

498. "...Tengamos fe en que la razón hace la fuerza, y en esa fe, atrevámonos hasta el fin a cumplir con nuestro deber como lo entendemos"... Abraham Lincoln. O. Bosch. Cortesía: Joyería Le Trianon, Central Shopping Plaza, Miami, Fla.,

1977.
Color; 48.3 x 63.5 cm.
C-P683F44:M5A713B6/f-1 no. 2

499. 3 Congreso Nacional, agosto 2-5, 1973, Abdala el futuro
      será nuestro. Clausura, domingo 5 de agosto 4 p.m. Ada
      Merrit High School. [Miami, Fla., 1973?]
      Color; 28 x 22 cm.
      C87-2-PO-9

500. Terrorismo global. 3er Congreso de Intelectuales Cubanos
      Disidentes. Institucionalización del terrorismo como
      instrumento en la internacionalización de la política
      exterior del gobierno cubano. Febrero 25-27, 1982.
      Georgetown University. Omar '82 / Design by P. Sierra.
      Washington D.C.: Comité de Intelectuales por la Libertad
      de Cuba, 1982.
      Color; 71.0 x 57.0 cm.
      C-P683F44:M5C8C713I5/f-1 no. 3

501. "Testimony for some day". Víctor. [Autographed. No. 56 of
      400]. Miami, Fla. : Little Havana Arts & Crafts Center,
      1981.
      Sepia; 53.3 x 73.2 cm.
      C-P683F44:M5A713G6/f-1 no. 1

502. The Third Miami Film Festival, For the love of film.
      Gusman Center for the Performing Arts. Coconut Grove
      Playhouse. February 7-16, 1986. Poster sponsorship:
      Publix Supermarkets, Inc. Artist: Humberto Calzada.
      [Miami, Fla.], 1986.
      Color; 85.1 x 56 cm.
      C-P683F44:M5A713C3/f-1 no. 4

503. 13th Anniversary. Hispanic Heritage Festival... October
      4-20, 1985. Aldo Amador, winner of 1985 Poster Contest.
      [Miami, Fla.] : The Miami Herald Pub. Co., 1985.
      Color; 63.5 x 48.3 cm.
      C-P683F44:M5F4H5/f-1 no. 3

504. Three Kings Day Parade. January 11, 1987. WQBA, 1140 kcs.
      La Cubanísima. City of Miami. [Artist] : Aldo Amador.
      [Miami, Fla.], 1987.
      Color; 62.3 x 44.0 cm.
      C-P683F44:M5P213T3/f-1 no. 1

505. To the democratic countries of the Western Hemisphere! Wake
      up!... United we are strong! We must belong to a new order.
      [Miami, Fla., n.d.]
      Color; 29.0 x 21.1 cm.
      C-P683F44:M5A513/f-1 no. 2

506. Tocla Productions presenta el Show de Charytín. Dade County
     Auditorium, sábado, agosto 21-domingo, agosto 22. Actuación
     especial de Lolita Berrio. [Miami, Fla., n.d.]
     B&w; 64.0 x 48.2 cm.
     C-P683F44:M5C8C613/f-2 no. 18

507. "Todos necesitamos el Finlay Total Care Plan", dicen Olga y
     Tony. Finlay HMO Total Care Plan... [Miami, Fla., n.d.]
     Color; 51.0 x 38.0 cm.
     C-P683F44:M5H413/f-1 no. 3

508. Los 3 grandes del feeling en concierto. Copacabana Supper
     Club... Domingo 4 diciembre... [Miami, Fla.] : Twin
     Printing, [n.d.]
     Color; 43.0 x 27.8 cm.
     C-P683F44:M5N513C6/f-1 no. 2

509. Trova Cubana del Exilio. Concierto en homenaje al
     natalicio de José Martí, 29 enero de 1988. [Artist]: Olga
     García. [Miami, Fla.], 1988.
     B&w; 57.0 x 38.5 cm.
     C-P683F44:M5M46H613/f-1 no. 1

510. 26-27 March 1977 Cuban Women's Club, Inc. Non-profit
     organization, member of Dade County Federation of Women's
     Clubs. Arte y artesanías. "The Hunter". Chris Miranda.
     [Miami, Fla.: Cuban Women's Club], 1977.
     B&w; 43.0 x 28.0 cm.
     C-P683F44:M5C8A713/f-1 no. 4

511. UCE. Reflejos, moda y color. Hotel San Juan, 4 de
     noviembre de 1988, 11:00 A.M. [San Juan, P.R.: U.C.E.],
     1988.
     Color; 58.7 x 42.0 cm.
     C-P633P81:F213/f-1 no. 1

512. Unete a la Cadena de la Democracia. Para Cuba ya es hora,
     José Martí. Febrero 24, 1990. [Miami, Fla.: Cadena de la
     Democracia], 1990.
     C-P683F44:M5F713C3/f-1 no. 1

513. An unforgetable evening of music, voice and art. Art: an
     exhibition of fine art and sculpture by the Metropolitan
     Museum and Art Centers. Opera: The Young Patronesses of
     the Opera will present two outstanding opera artists...
     Ballet: The Miami Ballet Society will present two
     performances. Classical guitar: Traditional and classical
     guitar presented by Centro Mater. [Miami, Fla., n.d.]
     Color; 30.4 x 25.4 cm.
     C-P683F44:M5C8M813/f-1 no. 1

514. United Cerebral Palsy, tele-maratón nacional, fín de semana con las estrellas. WPLG Canal 10, enero 17 y 18, 1987. Ayude a los niños con paralisis cerebral, ellos te necesitan!... Esperando la generosa contribución de la colonia latina de Miami... [Miami, Fla.], 1987.
Color; 48.0 x 33.0 cm.
C-P683F44:M5R313/f-1 no. 1

515. United in Heritage. The Miami-Dade Community College-South Hispanic Heritage Celebration. MDCC-South Campus, October 5, 6, 10. Charles III, Florida and the Gulf, An international humanities conference on the bicentennial of the death of King Charles III of Spain. Hotel Intercontinental, Miami, October 6-8. Sponsored by The Count of Galvez Historical Society, Inc... Graphic design: Jorge Martell... Miami, Fla.: Trade Litho, Inc., 1988].
Color; 84.7 x 56.5 cm.
C-P683F44:M5F4H5/f-2 no. 12

516. U.S. Hispanic omnibus. In the small towns and great cities of America, Greyhound and Trailways take you where you want to go , at a low fare... Calendar of Hispanic events and holiday... [New York] : Strategy Research Corporation, 1986.
Color; 62.5 x 42.2 cm.
C-P681:F303/f-1 no. 1

517. Universidad de Miami Teatro 66. 1era. temporada de teatro: cubano, hispano, americano. Mundo de cristal (The Glass Menagerie). Autor: Tennessee Williams. Con: Luis Molina, Nismi Nazar, Norma Acevedo, Salvador Ugarte... Estreno: 30 de abril, 8:30 p.m. Mayo 6-7, 13-14... Koubek Center. División Educación Continuada. Patronato del Teatro. [Miami, Fla., 1966].
Color; 51.0 x 35.6 cm.
C-P683F44:M5T613U5K6/f-1 no. 1

518. Vagabunda, por Mary Calleiro. Ilustraciones: Nelson Franco. "En la fantasía de su verso, revela las realidades de sus vivencias, con gran intensidad. Se descubre la sensibilidad de la artista y de la mujer," Alvaro Sánchez Cifuentes. [Miami, Fla.: SIBI, 1988].
B&w; 40.6 x 28.6 cm.
C-P683F44:M5M413B6/f-1 no. 8

519. 20 de mayo. Cubano marcha a Washington, D.C., defiende tu soberanía. Hotel Woodstock... martes y viernes. 5.30-7.30. [New Jersey, 1972].
B&w; 38.2 x 28 cm.
C87-2-PO-6

520. 28 de enero, 1978, acto conmemorativo, natalicio de Martí, X aniversario de la Agrupación Abdala... [Miami, FL, 1978.] B&w; 43 x 28 cm. C87-2-PO-21

521. Velada patriótica 126 aniversario del natalicio de José Martí, Koubek Center... enero 27, 1979, 8:00 p.m., Abdala. [Miami, Fla., 1979.] B&w; 27 x 20.5 cm. C87-2-PO-22

522. ¡Venga a disfrutar desde hoy con nuestro próximo regreso a la patria! ¡A Cuba me voy hoy mismo..., que se acabó el comunismo! Original de Alfonso Cremata & Salvador Ugarte. ¡La comedia que todo el exilio esperaba!... Teatro "Las Mascaras" #2... Funciones: viernes y sábado, 9:00 p.m. domingo, 5:00 y 8:00 p.m. [Miami, Fla., 1990]. Color; 44.2 x 29.0 cm. C-P683F44:M5T513M3/f-1 no. 6

523. La Verbena del 23, lo nuestro. Domingo, abril 5. Abril 2-5, Festival de Primavera de Hialeah. Entrada gratis. [Hialeah, Fla., n.d.] Color; 61.0 x 40.5 cm. C-P683F44:H5F4F37/f-1 no. 1

524. Víctor Manuel, un innovador en la pintura cubana. Inauguración Museo Cubano de Arte y Cultura. 10 de octubre de 1982... [Artist]: M. Ponce. [Miami, Fla.: Cuban Museum of Art and Culture], 1982. Color; 81.0 x 59.0 cm. C-P683F44:M5M813M8/f-1 no. 2

525. Video Casa presenta: La Cuba de ayer ¡El Paraíso que el comunismo convirtió en infierno! Actuación de Garrido y Piñero... Director: Manuel Alonso [y] Cuba satélite 13. Guión y dirección: Manuel de la Pedrosa... Productor: Eduardo Palmer... [Miami, Fla.: Video Casa TM, 1987?] Color; 61.2 x 24.8 cm. C-P683F44:M5V513/f-1 no. 2

526. Video Casa presenta "3 Patines en acción", con Leopoldo Fernández y Ernesto Albán... Dirección de Leopoldito Fernández y Manny San Fernando. Productor: Manolo C. Torres. Productor ejecutivo: Danilo Bardisa... [Artist] : Roblán. [Miami, Fla.] : Video Casa TM, 1980. Color; 61.2 x 45.6 cm. C-P683F44:M5V513/f-1 no. 1

527. Les Violins Supper Club presents "Havana Carnaval" enjoy the excitement, joy and rythm of old Havana. The most

spectacular floor show in our 20 year history!... [Artist]:
Del Pozo [Miami, Fla., 1980?]
Color; 30.5 x 21.5 cm.
C-P683F44:M5N513V5/f-1 no. 1

528. Virgen de la Caridad ¡Ruega por tus hijos! Fiesta de la
Virgen de la Caridad, martes 8 de septiembre. Misa solemne
en el gimnasio municipal (Coliseíto) a las 8:00 p.m...
Diseño: Rogelio Zelada. [San Juan, P.R.] : Unión de
Cubanos en el Exilio, 1987.
Color; 60.3 x 45.7 cm.
C-P633P81:R4P41308/f-1 no. 2

529. Virgen de la Caridad. Salva a Cuba! [Miami, Fla., 1990?]
Color; 53.5 x 49.6 cm.
C-P683F44:M5R4P41308/f-1 no. 5

530. Virgen mambisa ¡Reina de tu pueblo! 1936-Cincuentenario,
1986 de ser coronada reina y señora del pueblo cubano, 70
años de proclamada patrona de Cuba por Benedicto XV a
petición de nuestros libertadores. Fiesta de la Virgen de
la Caridad, lunes 8 de septiembre. Misa solemne en el
gimnasio municipal (Coliseíto) a las 8 p.m. Diseño:
Rogelio Zelada. Foto de la Virgen: Alberto Ortega. [San
Juan, P.R.]: Hermandad de Nuestra Señora de la Caridad,
1986.
Color; 61.0 x 45.5 cm.
C-P633P81:R4P41308/f-1 no. 1

531. Virgencita de la Caridad Patrona de Cuba te rogamos con
fervor que nos devuelvas a nuestra patria ultrajada.
Añorada Cuba.Diciembre 30, 8:00pm... Dade County
Auditorium... 25 aniversario. "S" printing, Sazón Goya,
WQBA La cubanisima, WLTV 23 Lo nuestro, Diario Las
Américas, Super Q fm 107.5. [Miami, Fla., 1989].
Color; 43.3 x 57.2 cm.
C-P683F44:M5S413A5/f-1 no. 4

532. Virgencita de la Caridad, patrona de cuba, te rogamos con
fervor que nos devuelvas a nuestra patria ultrajada. 25
Aniversario Añorada Cuba, febrero 25, 2:00 p.m. Dade
County Auditorium... [Miami, Fla., 1989].
Color; 57.0 x 43.5 cm.
C-P683F44:M5S413A5/f-1 no. 2

533. Vote Masvidal. Masvidal for mayor. Paid for "Masvidal
Campaign Fund". A. Codina, Treasurer. [Miami, Fla., 1987].
Color; 43.0 x 28.0 cm.
C-P683F44:M5P513M34/f-1 no. 1

534. Vote Masvidal #90. Paid for by "Masvidal Campaign fund".

A. Codina, Treasurer. [Miami, Fla., 1987].
Color; 43.0 x 28.0 cm.
C-P683F44:M5P513M34/f-1 no. 2

535. WCMQ (AM 1220) y FM 92 le da la bienvenida a Arie Kaduri en
la presentación de Lissette y Chirino en concierto, Dade
County Auditorium, sábado, noviembre 29. Una sola
presentación. [Miami, Fla., n.d.]
B&w; 43.2 x 27.8 cm.
C-P683F44:M5C8C613/f-1 no. 6

536. WRHC Cadena Azul, Old Milwaukee presentan Calle Ocho '88,
domingo 13 de marzo, calle 8 y 12 Court. Música por:
Continental Brass y Los Profesionales... Graphic design:
Jorge Martell. [Miami, Fla.] : Printed by Litho Inc.,
1988.
Color; 66.2 x 40.5 cm.
C-P683F44:M5F4C3/f-4 no. 40

537. When prison ships froze on the way to the Siberian mines...
nobody listened. When trains rolled heavily on the way to
the German extermination camps... nobody listened. When
Castro's jails crushed the cry of political prisoners...
nobody listened... the film by Néstor Almendros & Jorge
Ulla. For Academy Award consideration best documentary
feature. Winner IDA/1988 Distinguished Documentary
Achievement Award, International Documentary Association,
Los Angeles... Concept: Benito García. [Los Angeles,
Ca.] : Tribeca Typographers, Inc. 1988.
B&W; 46.7 x 28.7 cm.
C-P683F44:M5F513C2/f-1 no. 5

538. "The Word of Mouths." Frut gelato. [Artists: Jorge
Vallina and Pedro del Valle. Miami, Fla., 1982?]
Color; 57.5 x 41.0 cm.
C-P683F44:M5M413/f-1 no. 2

539. Y Tu... que haces por Cuba? Unete a la organización de tu
preferencia pero... únete! Masones Cubanos. Hialeah,
Fla., Respetable Logia Baire, [n.d.]
Color; 21.5 x 28.0 cm.
C-P683F44:M5L45C8/f-1 no. 8

540. Ya es hora! Llevemos a uno de los nuestros a comisionado
de Miami. Alfredo Durán Grupo 3, palanca 13-A. Si votamos
ganamos. Vota el martes 16... [Miami, Fla., n.d.]
B&w; 44.5 x 28.5 cm.
C-P683F44:M5P513C44/f-1 no. 2

541. Yo soy la Virgen de la Caridad. "Sabed que os estamos
siempre cercano... Paulus P.P. VI. [Artist] : Teok.

[Miami, Fla., n.d.]
Color; 31.9 x 25.8 cm.
C-P683F44:M5R4P41308/f-1 no. 3

542. Zilia Sánchez/Zilia Sánchez. Structures and prints, July 7-
31, 1970. [Miami, Fla.?], 1970.
B&w; 31.0 x 45.5 cm.
C-P683F44:M5C8A713/f-1 no. 2

SUBJECT INDEX

(Numbers refer to entries)

98

ARTIST INDEX

(Numbers refer to items)